Early Dunlop tire

A DK PUBLISHING BOOK

Project editor   Louise Pritchard
Art editor   Diane Clouting
Editor   Julie Ferris
Managing editor   Gillian Denton
Managing art editor   Julia Harris
Production   Charlotte Traill
Picture research   Jo Walton

First American Edition, 1996
2 4 6 8 10 9 7 5 3 1
Published in the United States by DK Publishing, Inc.
95 Madison Avenue, New York, NY 10016

Published in Great Britain by Dorling Kindersley Limited, London.

A CIP catalog record for this book is
available from the Library of Congress.

ISBN 0-7894-1022-2

Color reproduction by
Colourscan, Singapore
Printed in Italy by LEGO

Hindu snake demon mask

A cicada

A desert rose

Buff Orpington rooster

TOP 10 QUIZ BOOK

MERLO

Contents

Leaves from a ginkgo tree

Newspapers from around the world

The human body

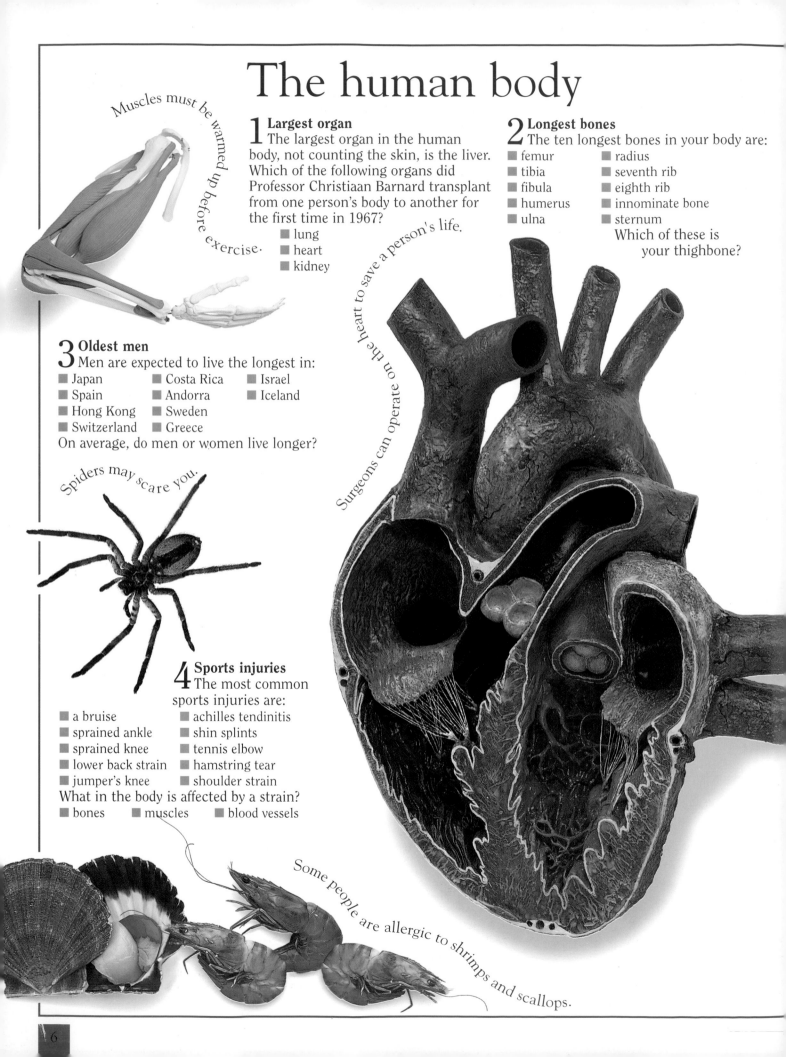

Muscles must be warmed up before exercise.

1 Largest organ
The largest organ in the human body, not counting the skin, is the liver. Which of the following organs did Professor Christiaan Barnard transplant from one person's body to another for the first time in 1967?
- lung
- heart
- kidney

2 Longest bones
The ten longest bones in your body are:
- femur
- tibia
- fibula
- humerus
- ulna
- radius
- seventh rib
- eighth rib
- innominate bone
- sternum

Which of these is your thighbone?

Surgeons can operate on the heart to save a person's life.

3 Oldest men
Men are expected to live the longest in:
- Japan
- Spain
- Hong Kong
- Switzerland
- Costa Rica
- Andorra
- Sweden
- Greece
- Israel
- Iceland

On average, do men or women live longer?

Spiders may scare you.

4 Sports injuries
The most common sports injuries are:
- a bruise
- sprained ankle
- sprained knee
- lower back strain
- jumper's knee
- achilles tendinitis
- shin splints
- tennis elbow
- hamstring tear
- shoulder strain

What in the body is affected by a strain?
- bones
- muscles
- blood vessels

Some people are allergic to shrimps and scallops.

5 Common accidents

The ten most common ways in which people are accidentally hurt at home are by:

- a fall
- cutting/piercing
- struck by a static object
- struck by a moving object
- foreign body
- burning
- jamming/pinching
- animal/insect bite
- poisoning
- over-exertion

With which of these medical instruments does a doctor look inside a person's body?

- stethoscope
- endoscope
- microscope

6 Visits to the doctor

Ten of the most common reasons why people visit the doctor are:

- breathing problems
- non-specific "symptoms"
- skin disorders
- mental problems
- high blood pressure
- rheumatic aches and pains
- stomach complaints
- minor accidents
- chronic rheumatism
- acute throat infections

The doctor on this page is testing for one of these ailments. Which one?

An endoscope is similar to a telescope.

The main bones in the leg are the femur, tibia, and fibula.

7 Common reaction

Some people have an unpleasant reaction to certain natural things around them.
The most common culprits are:

- house-dust mites
- weed pollen
- grass pollen
- wasp/bee venom
- tree pollen
- cats
- dogs
- horses
- molds
- birch pollen

Wasps and bees inject their venom into people with a stinger. Do both male and female wasps and bees sting?

8 Food reaction

Nuts are the food that causes the most people to have an unpleasant reaction. How do you describe an unpleasant reaction to food?

Wasps may sting several times.

9 Common fears

The ten most common things that seriously frighten people are:

- spiders
- people and social situations
- flying
- open spaces
- confined spaces
- heights
- cancer
- thunderstorms
- death
- vomiting

Which of these fears is called arachnophobia?

Doctors can listen to blood pumping through the body.

10 Longest-living women

Women are expected to live the longest in the following ten countries:

- Japan
- Australia
- Hong Kong
- Andorra
- France
- Martinique
- Iceland
- Switzerland
- Canada
- Spain

Is the average female life expectancy in these countries:

- more than 70 years
- more than 80 years
- more than 90 years

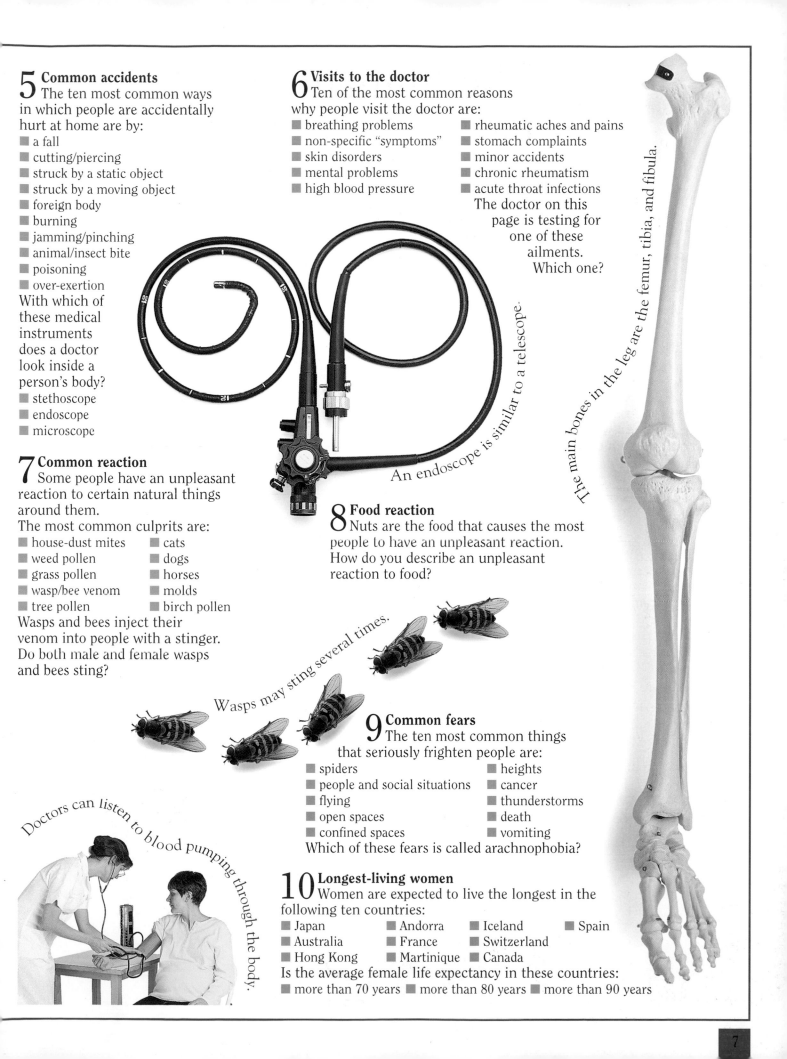

People

1 Female premiers
Sirimavo Bandaranaike, prime minister of Ceylon (now Sri Lanka) from 1960–64 and from 1970–77, was the first female prime minister in the world. Which of the following prime ministers was assassinated by her bodyguards in 1984?
- Margaret Thatcher (UK)
- Golda Meir (Israel)
- Indira Gandhi (India)

The Flying Doctor Service cares for people in the outback.

2 Longest reign
Louis XIV of France (1638–1715) remains the longest reigning monarch ever, with a reign of 72 years. What name is given to jeweled items owned by monarchs?

3 Wealthy people
The United States has more rich people than anywhere else. What are people with more than one million dollars or pounds called?

Royal crowns are encrusted with many jewels.

A portrait of emperor Tiberius decorates this scabbard.

4 Roman emperors
The first emperor of ancient Rome was Augustus. Which of these Roman emperors was Augustus' adopted son?
- Claudius
- Tiberius
- Nero

5 First president
The first president of the United States was in office from 1789–97. Was he:
- Thomas Jefferson
- George Washington
- John Adams

6 Duty free
The duty-free products on which most money is spent are cigarettes, perfume, and alcohol. What does duty-free mean?

One million dollars

7 Stressful job
The most stressful US job is said to be that of president. What name is given to the president's wife?

8 Litter
Cigarette butts are the most common type of litter. Chewing gum is another common type of litter and is illegal in Singapore. Is this true?

9 Walking at work
The ten occupations that require the most walking on the job are:
- police officer
- postal worker
- TV reporter
- nurse
- doctor
- store clerk
- secretary
- actor
- public relations executive
- real estate agent

In which country do some doctors fly to work?

Indira Gandhi was prime minister of India.

10 Top of the world
The first mountaineer to climb to the top of Mt. Everest was Edmund Hillary. In what month of 1953 did he reach the top?

Food and drink

A label on a wine bottle identifies its vineyard.

1 Mushroom farming
The world's largest mushroom farm is in Pennsylvania. It produces 27,000 tons (24,500 tonnes) of mushrooms a year. Which country eats the most mushrooms per person?
■ France   ■ Japan   ■ Australia

2 Sweet tooth
Cuba is the top sugar-consuming nation in the world. From what plant does most sugar come?

3 Ice-cream nation
More ice-cream is consumed in the US than in any other nation. Which day of the week does the name of a mixture of ice cream, fruit, and syrup sound like?

Coffee beans are roasted then ground.

4 Cheese producer
The country that produces the most cheese is the United States. From what is cheese made?

An ice-cream sundae

5 Tea drinkers
The people of the Republic of Ireland drink the most tea. Which country grows the most tea?
■ India
■ Japan
■ South Africa

6 Food crops
The food crops produced in the largest amounts are:
■ sugarcane
■ wheat
■ rice
■ corn
■ potatoes
■ sugar beets
■ barley
■ cassava
■ sweet potatoes
■ soybeans
From which crop is most bread made?

Wheat is milled to make flour.

7 Fruit quantities
The fruits produced in the largest amounts are:
■ oranges   ■ mangoes
■ coconuts   ■ pineapples
■ apples   ■ pears
■ grapes   ■ peaches
■ bananas   ■ nectarines
What is inside every fruit that will grow into a new plant?

8 Coffee drinkers
More coffee is consumed per person in Finland than in any other nation. Coffee is made from the leaves of the coffee tree. Is this true?

9 Oldest cake
The world's oldest cake is more than 4,000 years old. It was baked in ancient Egypt. Where was it found?
■ in a house
■ in a grave
■ in a temple

10 Expensive wine
The most expensive bottle of wine ever sold at auction was a 1787 Château Lafite. It sold for £105,000. In which country is Château Lafite made?

Some fruits have more than one seed.

Art and culture

Pocket-sized TVs are now available.

1 Shakespeare's longest
Shakespeare's ten longest plays are:

- *Hamlet*
- *Richard III*
- *Coriolanus*
- *Cymbeline*
- *Othello*
- *Antony and Cleopatra*
- *Troilus and Cressida*
- *Henry VIII*
- *Henry V*
- *The Winter's Tale*

What is the name of the theater in London where many of Shakespeare's plays were first performed?
- National Theatre ■ Swan Theatre ■ Globe Theatre

2 Youngest Oscar winners
The ten youngest Oscar winners ever are:

- Shirley Temple
- Margaret O'Brien
- Vincent Winter
- Jon Whitely
- Ivan Jandl
- Tatum O'Neal
- Anna Paquin
- Claude Jarman, Jr.
- Bobby Driscoll
- Hayley Mills

How old was Shirley Temple when she received her award in 1934?
- four ■ six ■ ten

Newspapers come in different sizes.

3 Top-selling album
The top-selling album worldwide is *Thriller*, which has sold more than 40 million copies. Whose album is it?

4 Best-seller
The world's best-selling book of all time is the Bible, with more than 6,000 million copies sold. It has been printed in more than 2,000 languages and dialects. What is special about the Gutenberg Bible, printed in 1455?

The first two Penguin paperback titles

The original Globe Theatre was destroyed by fire in 1613, during a performance of Henry VIII.

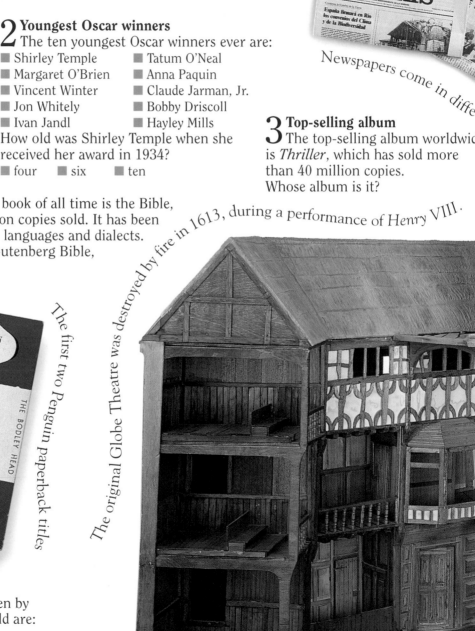

5 Popular language
The ten languages spoken by the most people in the world are:

- Mandarin
- English
- Hindustani
- Spanish
- Russian
- Arabic
- Bengali
- Portuguese
- Malay-Indonesian
- Japanese

In which country is Mandarin spoken?

Compact discs are much smaller than records.

6 Best-selling newspapers

The ten best-selling daily newspapers in the world are:

- *Yomiuri Shimbun*, Japan
- *Asahi Shimbun*, Japan
- *People's Daily*, China
- *Bild Zeitung*, Germany
- *The Sun*, UK
- *Daily Mirror*, UK
- *Wall Street Journal*, US
- *Daily Mail*, UK
- *USA Today*, US
- *Daily Express*, UK

What is the difference between a tabloid and a broadsheet newspaper?

7 Top animation

The ten most successful animated films are:

- *The Lion King*
- *The Jungle Book*
- *Toy Story*
- *Casper*
- *Aladdin*
- *Who Framed Roger Rabbit?*
- *Snow White and the Seven Dwarfs*
- *Beauty and the Beast*
- *Pocahontas*
- *One Hundred and One Dalmatians*

Which of these animated films is based on a true story?

8 Priceless painting

The highest price paid for a painting is $75,000,000 (£44,378,696). It was paid at an auction in New York for *Portrait of Dr. Gachet,* by Vincent van Gogh. Dr. Gachet was van Gogh's physician. Is this true?

The first books were written by hand.

9 Largest library

The largest library in the world is the Library of Congress in Washington, DC. It contains about 29 million books. What is a book with a soft cover called?

Animated films take a long time to make.

10 First television service

The first ten countries to have had a television broadcasting service were:

- UK
- Brazil
- Argentina
- US
- Cuba
- Denmark
- USSR
- Mexico
- Netherlands
- France

Who invented the television?

- John Logie Baird
- Guglielmo Marconi
- Heinrich Hertz

Transportation

1 Longest ship
The ten longest passenger ships are:
- Monarch of the Seas
- Majesty of the Seas
- Sovereign of the Seas
- Ecstasy
- Oriana
- QEII
- France
- Sensation
- Fantasy
- Canberra

What are large passenger ships called?

Some ocean liners carry more than 2,000 passengers.

Electric current flows through spark plugs in a car engine.

2 Best-seller
The ten top-selling motor vehicle manufacturers in the world are:
- General Motors
- Ford Motor Company
- Toyota
- Volkswagen
- Nissan
- PSA (Peugeot-Citroen)
- Renault
- Chrysler
- Mitsubishi
- Honda

Who invented the pneumatic (air-filled) tire?
- John Michelin
- John Dunlop
- John Goodyear

3 Longest rail network
The ten longest rail networks in the world are in:
- US
- Russia
- Canada
- China
- India
- Germany
- Australia
- France
- Argentina
- Brazil

In which of these countries can the largest railroad station be found?

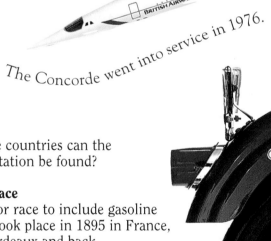

The Concorde went into service in 1976.

4 First car
The first successful gas-driven car was built by Karl-Friedrich Benz and first ran in 1885. What lights the fuel in a car engine to make it work?

5 First motor race
The first motor race to include gasoline engine vehicles took place in 1895 in France, from Paris to Bordeaux and back. Which Italian car company is famous for its red race cars?

Most locomotives are diesel powered.

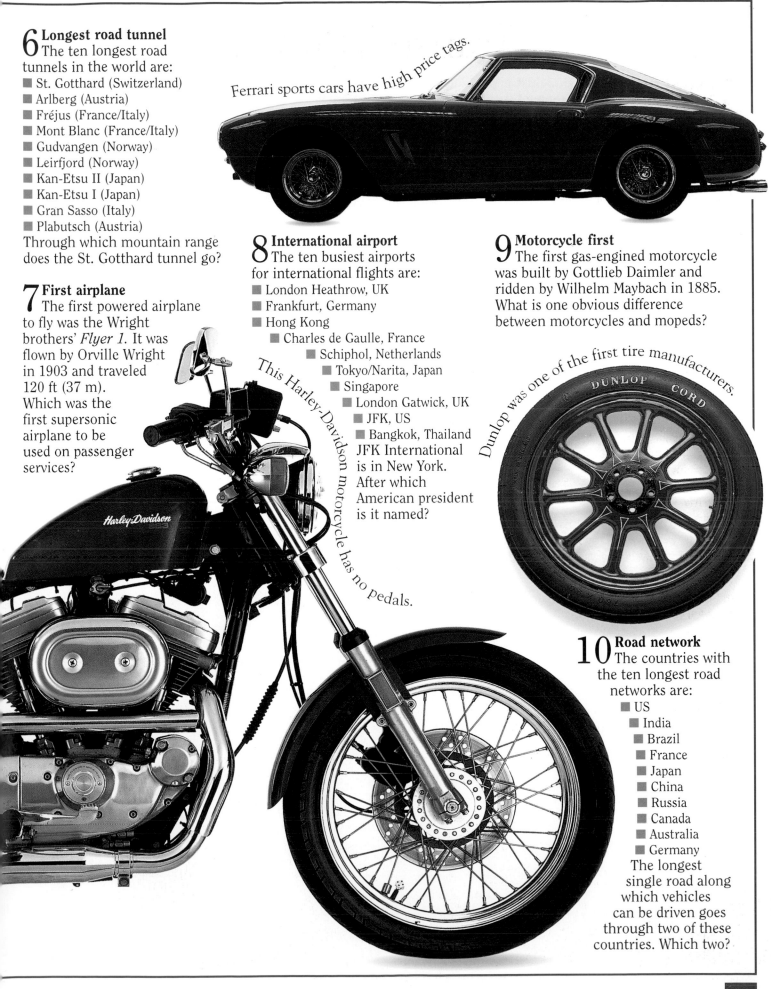

6 Longest road tunnel
The ten longest road tunnels in the world are:
- St. Gotthard (Switzerland)
- Arlberg (Austria)
- Fréjus (France/Italy)
- Mont Blanc (France/Italy)
- Gudvangen (Norway)
- Leirfjord (Norway)
- Kan-Etsu II (Japan)
- Kan-Etsu I (Japan)
- Gran Sasso (Italy)
- Plabutsch (Austria)

Through which mountain range does the St. Gotthard tunnel go?

7 First airplane
The first powered airplane to fly was the Wright brothers' *Flyer 1*. It was flown by Orville Wright in 1903 and traveled 120 ft (37 m). Which was the first supersonic airplane to be used on passenger services?

Ferrari sports cars have high price tags.

8 International airport
The ten busiest airports for international flights are:
- London Heathrow, UK
- Frankfurt, Germany
- Hong Kong
- Charles de Gaulle, France
- Schiphol, Netherlands
- Tokyo/Narita, Japan
- Singapore
- London Gatwick, UK
- JFK, US
- Bangkok, Thailand

JFK International is in New York. After which American president is it named?

This Harley-Davidson motorcycle has no pedals.

9 Motorcycle first
The first gas-engined motorcycle was built by Gottlieb Daimler and ridden by Wilhelm Maybach in 1885. What is one obvious difference between motorcycles and mopeds?

Dunlop was one of the first tire manufacturers.

10 Road network
The countries with the ten longest road networks are:
- US
- India
- Brazil
- France
- Japan
- China
- Russia
- Canada
- Australia
- Germany

The longest single road along which vehicles can be driven goes through two of these countries. Which two?

Religion

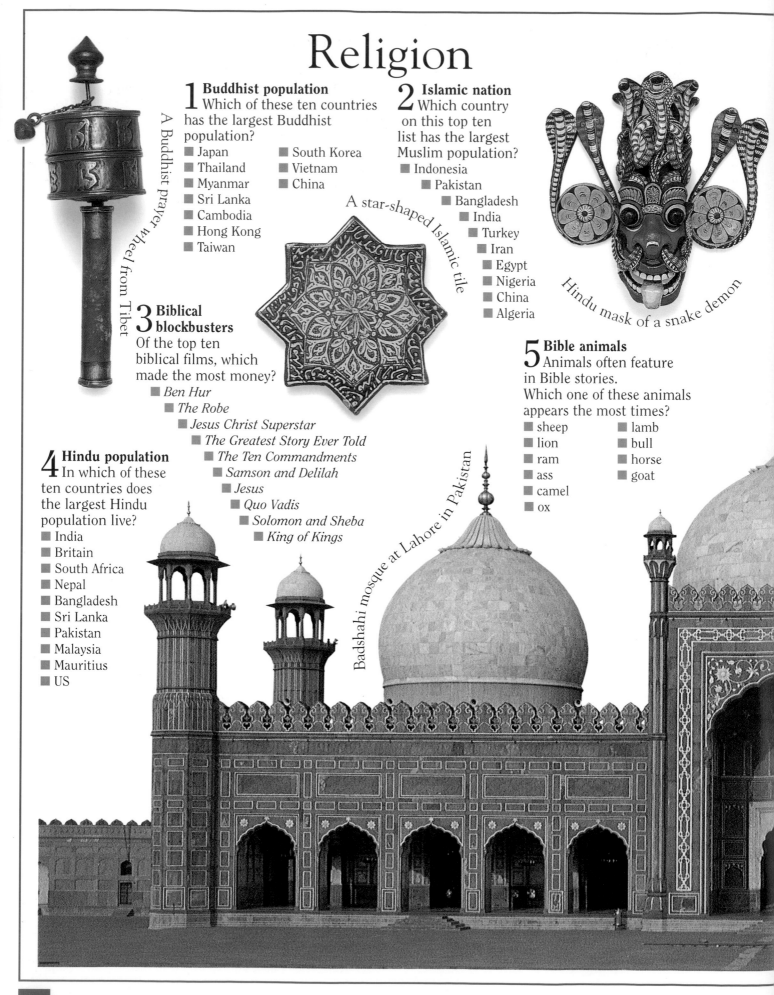

1 Buddhist population
Which of these ten countries has the largest Buddhist population?
- Japan
- South Korea
- Thailand
- Vietnam
- Myanmar
- China
- Sri Lanka
- Cambodia
- Hong Kong
- Taiwan

A Buddhist prayer wheel from Tibet

2 Islamic nation
Which country on this top ten list has the largest Muslim population?
- Indonesia
- Pakistan
- Bangladesh
- India
- Turkey
- Iran
- Egypt
- Nigeria
- China
- Algeria

A star-shaped Islamic tile

Hindu mask of a snake demon

3 Biblical blockbusters
Of the top ten biblical films, which made the most money?
- *Ben Hur*
- *The Robe*
- *Jesus Christ Superstar*
- *The Greatest Story Ever Told*
- *The Ten Commandments*
- *Samson and Delilah*
- *Jesus*
- *Quo Vadis*
- *Solomon and Sheba*
- *King of Kings*

4 Hindu population
In which of these ten countries does the largest Hindu population live?
- India
- Britain
- South Africa
- Nepal
- Bangladesh
- Sri Lanka
- Pakistan
- Malaysia
- Mauritius
- US

5 Bible animals
Animals often feature in Bible stories. Which one of these animals appears the most times?
- sheep
- lamb
- lion
- bull
- ram
- horse
- ass
- goat
- camel
- ox

Badshahi mosque at Lahore in Pakistan

6 World religions
The top ten world religions are:
- Islam
- Jainism
- Judaism
- Sikhism
- Buddism
- Bahai'ism
- Christianity
- Hinduism
- Confucianism
- Shintoism

Which has the largest number of followers?

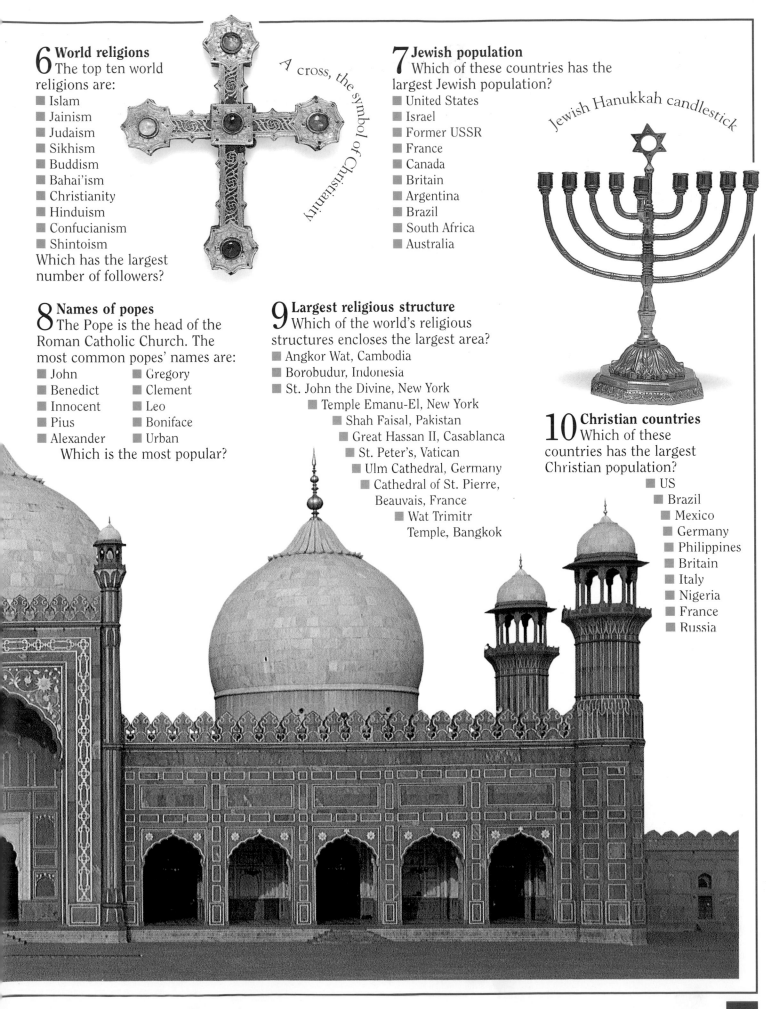

A cross, the symbol of Christianity

7 Jewish population
Which of these countries has the largest Jewish population?
- United States
- Israel
- Former USSR
- France
- Canada
- Britain
- Argentina
- Brazil
- South Africa
- Australia

Jewish Hanukkah candlestick

8 Names of popes
The Pope is the head of the Roman Catholic Church. The most common popes' names are:
- John
- Benedict
- Innocent
- Pius
- Alexander
- Gregory
- Clement
- Leo
- Boniface
- Urban

Which is the most popular?

9 Largest religious structure
Which of the world's religious structures encloses the largest area?
- Angkor Wat, Cambodia
- Borobudur, Indonesia
- St. John the Divine, New York
- Temple Emanu-El, New York
- Shah Faisal, Pakistan
- Great Hassan II, Casablanca
- St. Peter's, Vatican
- Ulm Cathedral, Germany
- Cathedral of St. Pierre, Beauvais, France
- Wat Trimitr Temple, Bangkok

10 Christian countries
Which of these countries has the largest Christian population?
- US
- Brazil
- Mexico
- Germany
- Philippines
- Britain
- Italy
- Nigeria
- France
- Russia

Extinct animals

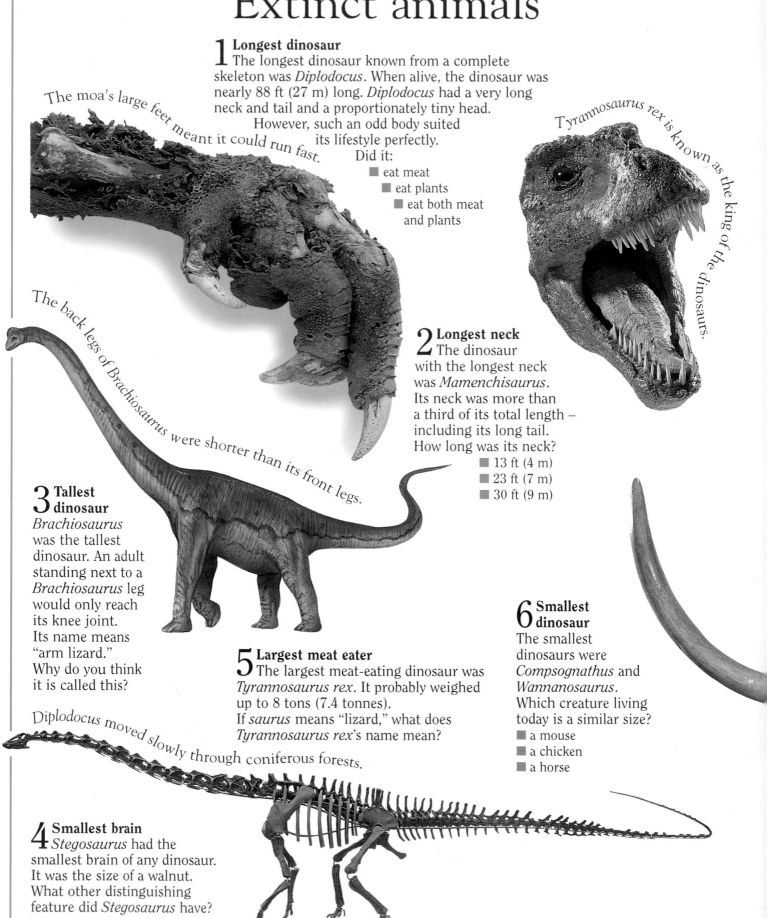

1 Longest dinosaur
The longest dinosaur known from a complete skeleton was *Diplodocus*. When alive, the dinosaur was nearly 88 ft (27 m) long. *Diplodocus* had a very long neck and tail and a proportionately tiny head. However, such an odd body suited its lifestyle perfectly.
Did it:
- eat meat
- eat plants
- eat both meat and plants

The moa's large feet meant it could run fast.

Tyrannosaurus rex is known as the king of the dinosaurs.

2 Longest neck
The dinosaur with the longest neck was *Mamenchisaurus*. Its neck was more than a third of its total length – including its long tail. How long was its neck?
- 13 ft (4 m)
- 23 ft (7 m)
- 30 ft (9 m)

The back legs of Brachiosaurus were shorter than its front legs.

3 Tallest dinosaur
Brachiosaurus was the tallest dinosaur. An adult standing next to a *Brachiosaurus* leg would only reach its knee joint. Its name means "arm lizard." Why do you think it is called this?

5 Largest meat eater
The largest meat-eating dinosaur was *Tyrannosaurus rex*. It probably weighed up to 8 tons (7.4 tonnes). If *saurus* means "lizard," what does *Tyrannosaurus rex*'s name mean?

6 Smallest dinosaur
The smallest dinosaurs were *Compsognathus* and *Wannanosaurus*. Which creature living today is a similar size?
- a mouse
- a chicken
- a horse

Diplodocus moved slowly through coniferous forests.

4 Smallest brain
Stegosaurus had the smallest brain of any dinosaur. It was the size of a walnut. What other distinguishing feature did *Stegosaurus* have?

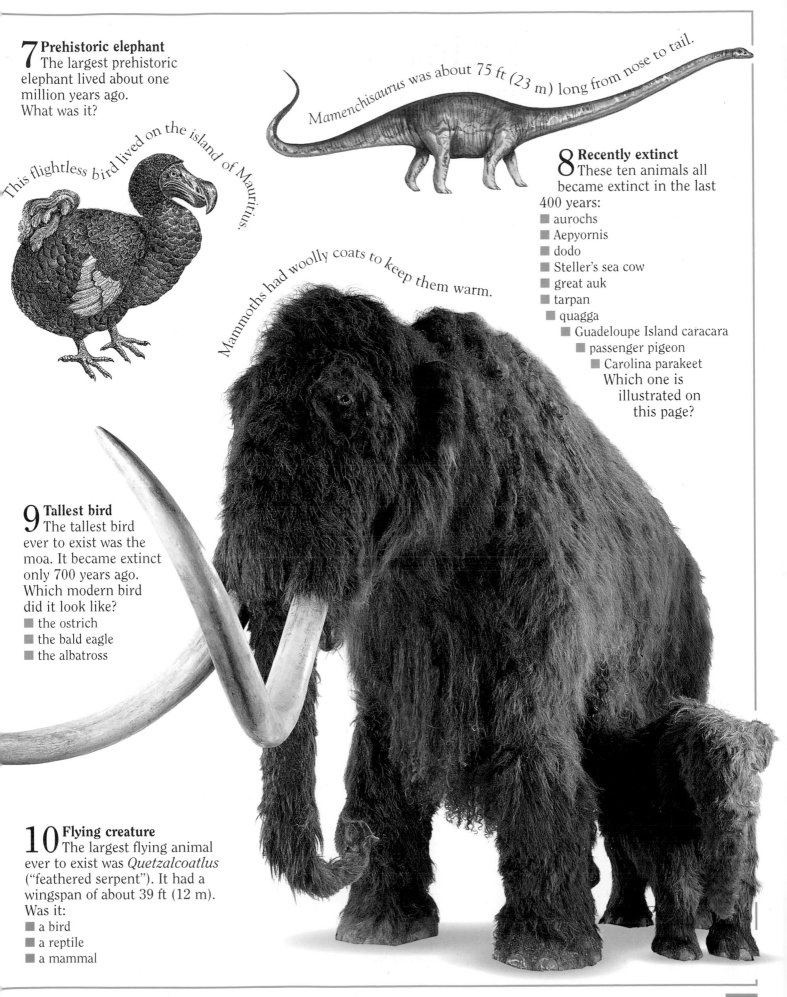

7 Prehistoric elephant
The largest prehistoric elephant lived about one million years ago. What was it?

This flightless bird lived on the island of Mauritius.

Mamenchisaurus was about 75 ft (23 m) long from nose to tail.

Mammoths had woolly coats to keep them warm.

8 Recently extinct
These ten animals all became extinct in the last 400 years:
■ aurochs
■ Aepyornis
■ dodo
■ Steller's sea cow
■ great auk
■ tarpan
■ quagga
   ■ Guadeloupe Island caracara
    ■ passenger pigeon
     ■ Carolina parakeet
Which one is illustrated on this page?

9 Tallest bird
The tallest bird ever to exist was the moa. It became extinct only 700 years ago. Which modern bird did it look like?
■ the ostrich
■ the bald eagle
■ the albatross

10 Flying creature
The largest flying animal ever to exist was *Quetzalcoatlus* ("feathered serpent"). It had a wingspan of about 39 ft (12 m). Was it:
■ a bird
■ a reptile
■ a mammal

Domestic animals

Julius Caesar remarked on the bravery of the mastiff.

A ragdoll cat completely relaxes when it is stroked.

1 Oldest horse
The greatest recorded age of a horse is 62. Which part of a horse would you look at to estimate its age?

2 Heaviest rooster
The heaviest type of domestic chicken is the male White Sully. A rooster can weigh up to 22 lb (10 kg). What is another name for a rooster?

3 Smallest horse
The smallest breed of horse is less than 30 in (76 cm) tall, smaller than a labrador dog. What is the breed?

4 Smallest dog
The smallest dog on record was a Yorkshire terrier, weighing only 4 oz (113 g). How tall was it at the shoulder?
◾ 2.5 in (6.3 cm)
◾ 4 in (10.3 cm)
◾ 6 in (15.3 cm)

Dwarf Netherland rabbits may weigh only 2 lb (0.9 kg).

A Buff Orpington rooster

5 Breeding like rabbits
New Zealand White and Californian rabbits have the most young, with up to 72 a year. What is a young rabbit called?

6 Top cat
The largest cat is the Ragdoll. It can weigh 20 lb (9 kg). Why is it called a Ragdoll?

7 Smallest pig
The smallest breed of domestic pig is the Mini Maialino. An adult male weighs only 20 lb (9 kg). What is a female Maialino called?

Lincoln Long-wool sheep are bred for their wool.

8 Heavy hound
The heaviest breeds of domestic dog are the mastiff and the St. Bernard. Males regularly weigh 170-200 lb (77-91 kg). Which of these was used in battle by the ancient Romans?

Pig litters can contain up to 20 piglets.

9 Sheep station
The largest sheep station in the world is in South Australia. How many sheep does it have?
◾ 7,000
◾ 17,000
◾ 70,000

10 Dwarf rabbit
The smallest breeds of domestic rabbit are the Netherland Dwarf and the Polish. They can weigh as little as 2 lb (0.9 kg). Are they larger or smaller than the smallest dog?

Birds

Answer the questions below by picking the correct bird from this list of ten:

- peregrine falcon
- great bustard
- crested argus
- ostrich
- kakapo
- bee hummingbird
- red-billed quelea
- Arctic tern
- wandering albatross
- oystercatcher

A peregrine falcon dives through the air to catch its prey.

The wandering albatross can measure 9.8 ft (3 m) from wing tip to wing tip.

Birds have different kinds of feathers for flying and to keep warm.

The Arctic tern flies 25,000 miles (40,000 km) every year.

The bee hummingbird is only 2.2 in (5.7 cm) long.

The flightless ostrich lays the largest eggs of all birds.

1 Largest feathers
Birds are the only animals with feathers. Which bird has the largest feathers?

2 Pet parrots
About 600,000 parrots are caught each year and sold as pets. Which parrot is the rarest bird in the world?

3 Songbirds
More than half the world's birds are known as songbirds. Which songbird is the most abundant bird of all?

4 Wingspan
Birds that glide over the sea on air currents have long narrow wings. Which seabird has the largest wingspan of any bird?

5 Big bird
Scientists believe that no bird heavier than 40 lb (18 kg), about the size of a large dog, could fly. Which is the largest flying bird?

6 Long life
Many birds living beside the sea use their long beaks to find food. Which shore bird is the longest-living wild bird?

7 Birds of prey
Most birds of prey have to move quickly to catch live, small animals to eat. Which bird of prey can reach the fastest speed?

8 Smallest bird
Birds exist in a huge range of body sizes. Which is the smallest bird in the world?

9 Largest bird
A few birds cannot fly at all because their wings are not designed for flight. Which flightless bird is the largest bird in the world?

10 Migration
Many birds migrate great distances every year to breed. Which bird makes the longest migratory journey of any animal?

Animal records

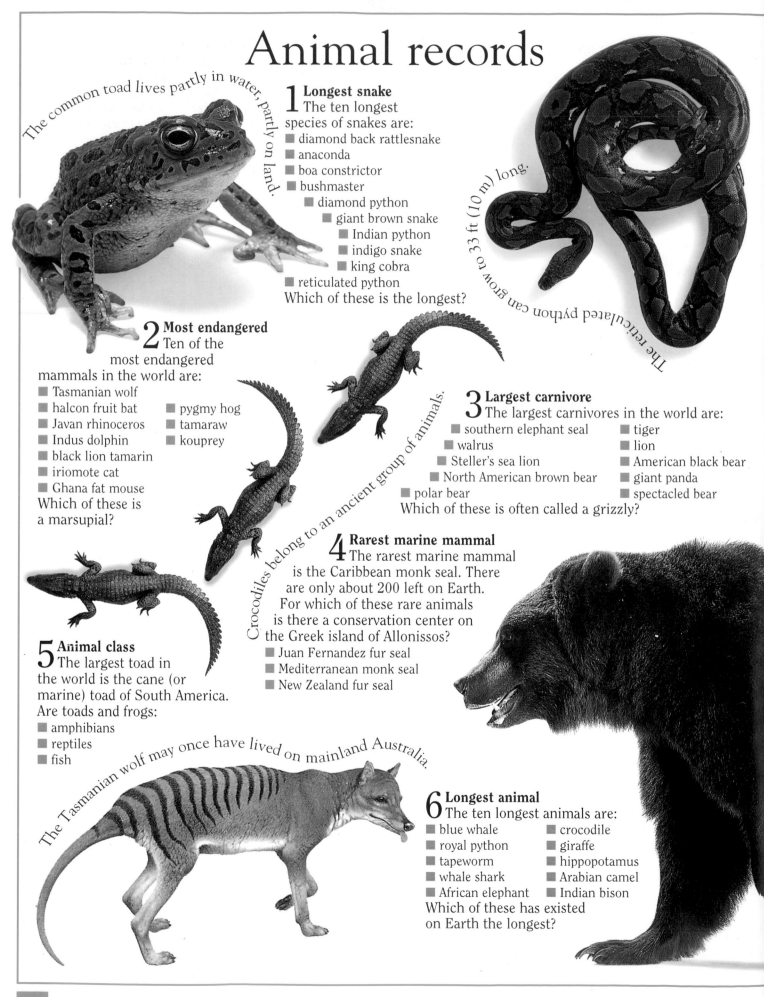

The common toad lives partly in water, partly on land.

1 Longest snake
The ten longest species of snakes are:
- diamond back rattlesnake
- anaconda
- boa constrictor
- bushmaster
- diamond python
- giant brown snake
- Indian python
- indigo snake
- king cobra
- reticulated python

Which of these is the longest?

The reticulated python can grow to 33 ft (10 m) long.

2 Most endangered
Ten of the most endangered mammals in the world are:
- Tasmanian wolf
- halcon fruit bat
- Javan rhinoceros
- Indus dolphin
- black lion tamarin
- iriomote cat
- Ghana fat mouse
- pygmy hog
- tamaraw
- kouprey

Which of these is a marsupial?

Crocodiles belong to an ancient group of animals.

3 Largest carnivore
The largest carnivores in the world are:
- southern elephant seal
- walrus
- Steller's sea lion
- North American brown bear
- polar bear
- tiger
- lion
- American black bear
- giant panda
- spectacled bear

Which of these is often called a grizzly?

4 Rarest marine mammal
The rarest marine mammal is the Caribbean monk seal. There are only about 200 left on Earth. For which of these rare animals is there a conservation center on the Greek island of Allonissos?
- Juan Fernandez fur seal
- Mediterranean monk seal
- New Zealand fur seal

5 Animal class
The largest toad in the world is the cane (or marine) toad of South America. Are toads and frogs:
- amphibians
- reptiles
- fish

The Tasmanian wolf may once have lived on mainland Australia.

6 Longest animal
The ten longest animals are:
- blue whale
- royal python
- tapeworm
- whale shark
- African elephant
- crocodile
- giraffe
- hippopotamus
- Arabian camel
- Indian bison

Which of these has existed on Earth the longest?

African hunting dogs live in family groups of about ten dogs.

7 Longest living
These ten animals live longer than any others, not including humans:

- marine clam
- giant tortoise
- Greek tortoise
- killer whale
- European eel
- lake sturgeon
- sea anemone
- elephant
- freshwater mussel
- Andean condor

Which one of these creatures lives on islands in the Indian Ocean?

An armadillo has bony plates growing in its skin.

8 Fastest mammal
The fastest mammal on land is the cheetah. How fast can it travel?

- 25 mph (40 km/h)
- 34 mph (55 km/h)
- 66 mph (105 km/h)

The giant tortoise has lost many of its natural habitats.

9 Largest litter
The ten mammals with the largest litters are:

- Malagasy tenrec
- Virginian opossum
- golden hamster
- ermine
- prairie vole
- coypu
- European hedgehog
- African hunting dog
- meadow vole
- wild boar

Which of these mammals hunts in a pack?

Many greyhounds are bred for racing.

The fur of some brown bears is tipped with silver.

10 Laziest creatures
The animals that sleep the most (not including those animals that hibernate) are:

- koala
- sloth
- armadillo
- opossum
- lemur
- hamster
- squirrel
- cat
- pig
- spiny anteater

The name of which animal means "little armored one"?

Mediterranean monk seals live among Aegean islands.

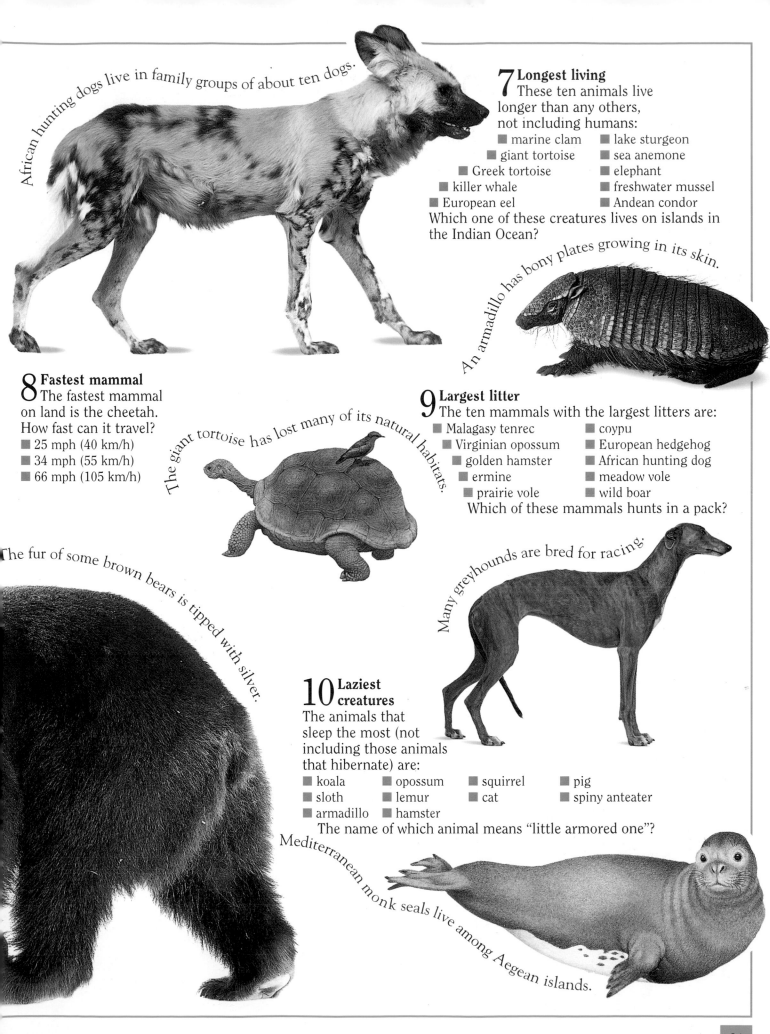

Insects and spiders

Cicadas use special areas on their bodies to communicate.

1 Loudest insect
The loudest insects of all are cicadas. The adult males make a noise to attract the females. Where are cicadas' ears?

2 Insect migration
The insect that migrates the longest distance is the painted lady butterfly. Do butterflies usually fly by day or by night?

The painted lady butterfly likes sunlight.

3 Largest insect
The largest insect is the Queen Alexandra birdwing butterfly of Papua New Guinea. It is also one of the rarest animals in the world. What is the name of the worldwide organization that campaigns to protect wildlife?

Spiders have eight legs.

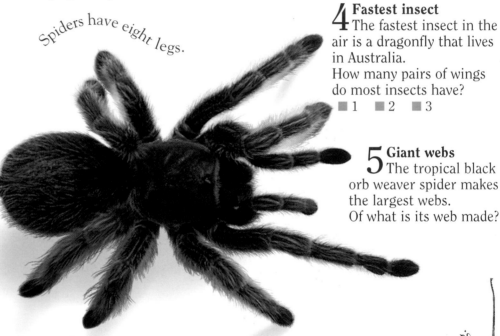

4 Fastest insect
The fastest insect in the air is a dragonfly that lives in Australia. How many pairs of wings do most insects have?
- 1
- 2
- 3

5 Giant webs
The tropical black orb weaver spider makes the largest webs. Of what is its web made?

6 Largest spider
The largest spider is the Goliath bird-eating spider. What is the most obvious difference between a spider and an insect?

7 Heaviest insect
The world's heaviest insect is the Goliath beetle of Africa. It weighs 4 oz (110 g), which is about the same as an apple. Can this huge beetle fly?

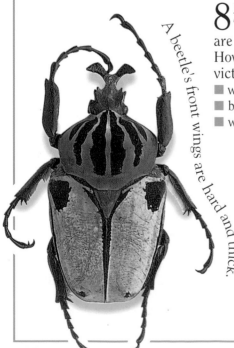

A beetle's front wings are hard and thick.

8 Most deadly
The most venomous spiders are Brazilian wandering spiders. How do spiders poison their victims?
- with a sting
- by scratching
- with a bite

9 Longest insect
The longest insect in the world is the giant stick insect from New Guinea. It has a long, thin body and slender legs. Why is it called a stick insect?

A stick insect can stay very still on a twig.

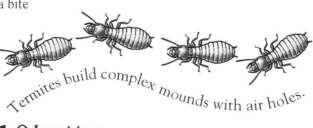

Termites build complex mounds with air holes.

10 Insect towers
The largest insect homes are termite mounds. They may house as many as five million insects. How do termites breathe inside the mound?

Reptiles

1 Longest lizard
The longest lizard is the Salvadori monitor of Papua New Guinea. It can grow up to 15.6 ft (4.75 m) long, of which 70 percent is its tail. What can many lizards do if a predator grabs them by the tail?

2 Fastest snake
The black mamba of tropical eastern Africa is the fastest snake. It can travel at nearly 12 mph (more than 19 km/h). How do most snakes move?

A flying gecko can grow a new tail.

Snakes form curves with their bodies.

3 Giant fangs
The snake with the longest fangs is the gaboon viper of tropical Africa. Its fangs can be as long as 2 in (5 cm). How does this snake kill its prey?
- by suffocation
- by swallowing it
- by poisoning it with venom

The chameleon sheds its skin from time to time.

5 Smallest reptile
The smallest reptile is a species of gecko that lives on the Virgin Islands. It is only 1.4 in (3.5 cm) long, about the size of your little finger. Is a gecko a lizard or a turtle?

6 Largest lizard
The Komodo dragon of Indonesia is the largest lizard in the world. It can grow to more than 9.8 ft (3 m) in length. Is it true that the Komodo dragon can kill and eat a pig?

4 Largest turtle
The largest turtle is the leatherback, which is more than 6.6 ft (2 m) long. What is unusual about this turtle's shell?

Turtles dig a hole for their eggs.

Crocodiles have large teeth with which to grab prey.

7 Egg laying
Sea turtles lay more eggs than any other reptile. They may lay up to 200 eggs in a single clutch. Where do they lay their eggs?

8 Old reptile
The longest-lived reptiles are species of giant tortoises. The oldest tortoise ever recorded came from the Seychelles. How old was it when it died?
- 52
- 125
- 152

9 Largest reptile
The largest reptile is the saltwater crocodile. It can grow to more than 23 ft (7 m) in length. In which watery habitat would you find most species of crocodiles?

10 Smallest snake
The smallest snake is the thread snake from the West Indies. It is less than 4.4 in (11 cm) long. Snakes and lizards grow throughout their lives. What happens to their skin as they grow?

Plant life

Santa Lucia fir trees have long, sharp, needlelike leaves.

1 Deadly fungus
The death cap is the most deadly fungus in the world.
How long would it take to kill you?
- 6–15 hours
- 3–6 days
- 1–3 weeks

A coco-de-mer seed takes 10 years to develop.

Insects are attracted to rafflesia flowers by their smell.

2 Tallest grass
Bamboo is the tallest type of grass. It grows up to 130 ft (40 m) high, taller than a ten-story building. Which black and white animal is famous for eating bamboo?

4 Largest seed
The largest seed of any plant can weigh up to 44 lb (20 kg), as much as an average five-year-old child. This plant only grows in the Seychelles Islands.
What is its seed?
- a coconut
- a coco-de-mer
- a cacao seed

5 Seaweed leaves
Pacific giant kelp is the seaweed with the longest fronds. They can grow to 197 ft (60 m) long.
How many adult humans could lie along the length of one frond?
- more than 35
- more than 45
- more than 65

3 Largest bloom
The rafflesia has the biggest flower. This broad, parasitic plant is found on the island of Sumatra. It grows to 3 ft (1 m) across.
Why do you think it is sometimes called the stinking corpse lily?

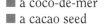

Trees are the largest land plants.

6 Largest fruiting body
The giant puffball grows the largest fruiting body, It can be as large as 6.5 ft (2 m) in circumference.
Is a puffball:
- ■ a seaweed
- ■ a shrub
- ■ a fungus

Ginkgo leaves hang down on long stalks.

7 Rare fir
The rarest North American native fir is the Santa Lucia fir. Do fir trees drop their leaves in the fall?

Sequoias are also known as redwoods.

Eucalyptus leaves contain oil that attracts koala bears.

8 Oldest species
The ginkgo is the oldest surviving species of tree. What else is it sometimes called?
- ■ the maidenhair tree
- ■ the mermaid's bower
- ■ the monsterleaf tree

9 Towering tree
The giant sequoia is the most massive species of tree. The most massive tree of all is called General Sherman. It has a diameter of 36.4 ft (11.1 m) and an estimated weight of 1968 tons (2,000 tonnes). It can be found in California.
Does a sequoia have cones or flowers?

10 Tallest species
The tallest species of tree is an eucalyptus found in the parched outback and forests of Australia. The trees can grow to higher than 374 ft (114 m), taller than the Statue of Liberty.
Is this true or false?

Earth

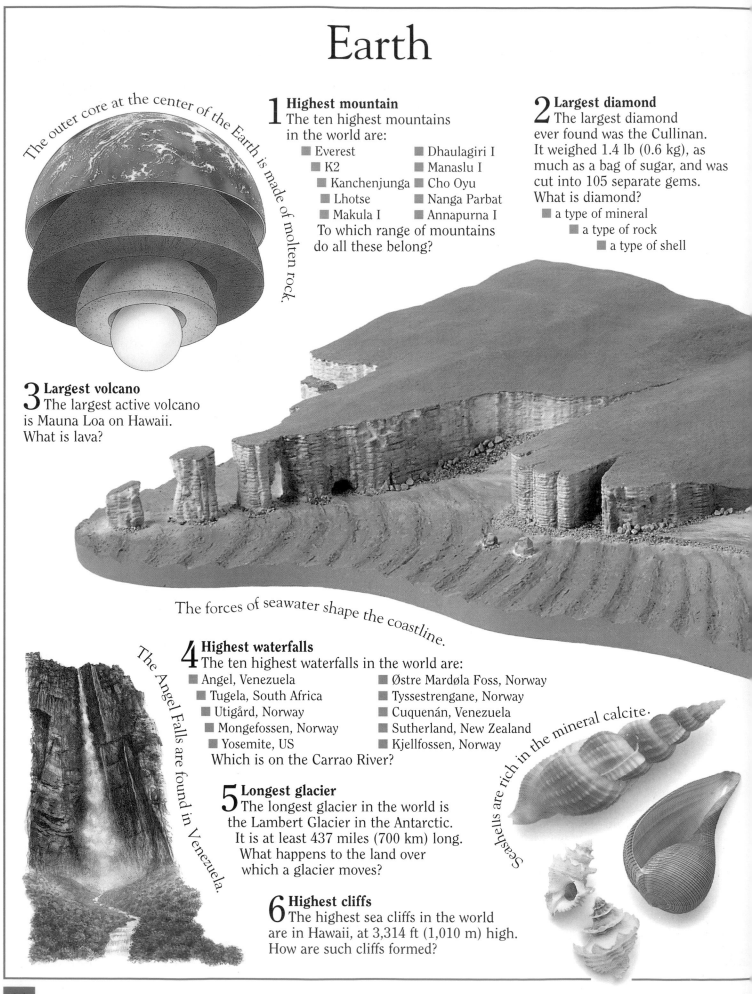

The outer core at the center of the Earth is made of molten rock.

1 Highest mountain
The ten highest mountains in the world are:

- Everest
- K2
- Kanchenjunga
- Lhotse
- Makula I
- Dhaulagiri I
- Manaslu I
- Cho Oyu
- Nanga Parbat
- Annapurna I

To which range of mountains do all these belong?

2 Largest diamond
The largest diamond ever found was the Cullinan. It weighed 1.4 lb (0.6 kg), as much as a bag of sugar, and was cut into 105 separate gems. What is diamond?

- a type of mineral
- a type of rock
- a type of shell

3 Largest volcano
The largest active volcano is Mauna Loa on Hawaii. What is lava?

The forces of seawater shape the coastline.

4 Highest waterfalls
The ten highest waterfalls in the world are:

- Angel, Venezuela
- Tugela, South Africa
- Utigård, Norway
- Mongefossen, Norway
- Yosemite, US
- Østre Mardøla Foss, Norway
- Tyssestrengane, Norway
- Cuquenán, Venezuela
- Sutherland, New Zealand
- Kjellfossen, Norway

Which is on the Carrao River?

The Angel Falls are found in Venezuela.

5 Longest glacier
The longest glacier in the world is the Lambert Glacier in the Antarctic. It is at least 437 miles (700 km) long. What happens to the land over which a glacier moves?

6 Highest cliffs
The highest sea cliffs in the world are in Hawaii, at 3,314 ft (1,010 m) high. How are such cliffs formed?

Seashells are rich in the mineral calcite.

7 Largest islands
The ten largest islands in the world are:
- Greenland
- New Guinea
- Borneo
- Madagascar
- Baffin Island
- Sumatra
- Honshu
- Great Britain
- Victoria Island
- Ellesmere Island

Is Greenland in the:
- Antarctic Ocean
- Arctic Ocean
- Atlantic Ocean

8 Longest rivers
The ten longest rivers in the world are:
- Nile, Africa
- Amazon, South America
- Yangtze–Kiang, China
- Mississippi–Missouri–Red Rock, US
- Yenisey–Angara-Selenga, Russian Federation
- Huang Ho (Yellow River), China
- Ob'–Irtysh, Russian Federation
- Zaire (Congo), Africa
- Lena–Kirenga, Russia
- Mekong, Asia

Which river is the longest?

Pinnacles in Bryce Canyon, in the US, were eroded by the weather.

Minerals form crystals when they solidify.

9 Largest gorge
The largest gorge is the Grand Canyon in Arizona cut into the rocks by the Colorado River. It is more than 279 miles (446 km) long, with an average width of 10 miles (16 km), and a depth of 1 mile (1.6 km).

What term is given to the wearing away of rocks?

When a glacier melts it leaves behind a wide U-shaped valley.

10 Deepest oceans
The deepest oceans and seas in the world are:
- Pacific Ocean
- Atlantic Ocean
- South China Sea
- Gulf of Mexico
- Japan Sea
- Indian Ocean
- Caribbean Sea
- Bering Sea
- Mediterranean Sea
- Arctic Ocean

Some rocks are made mostly from the remains of seashells. Is this true?

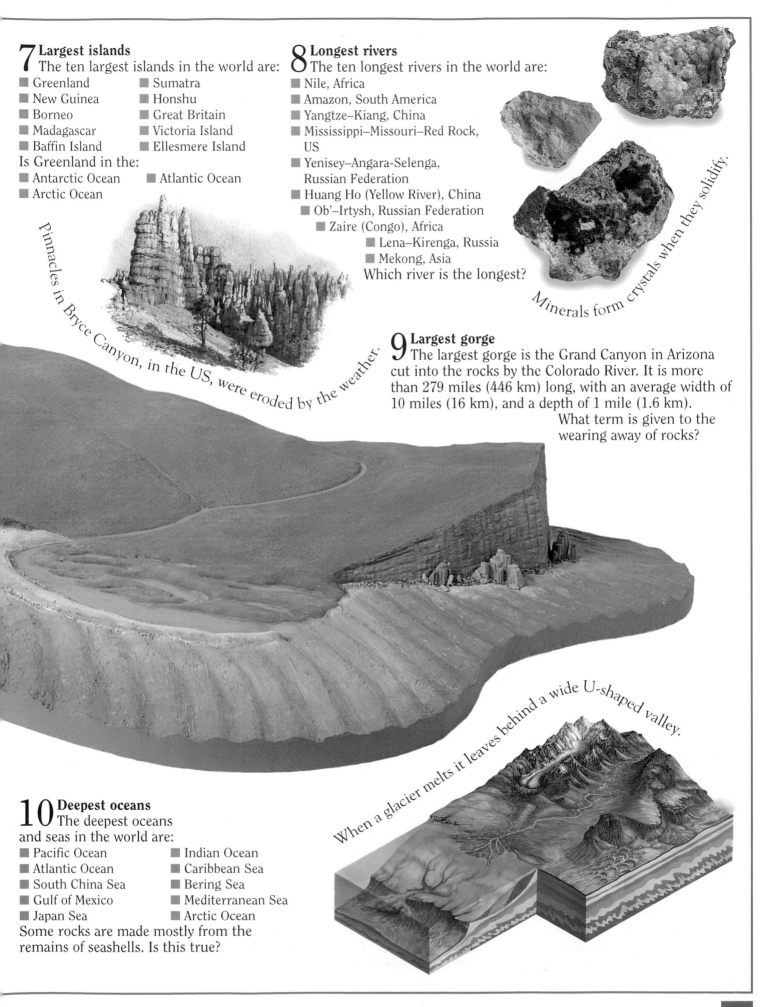

Space

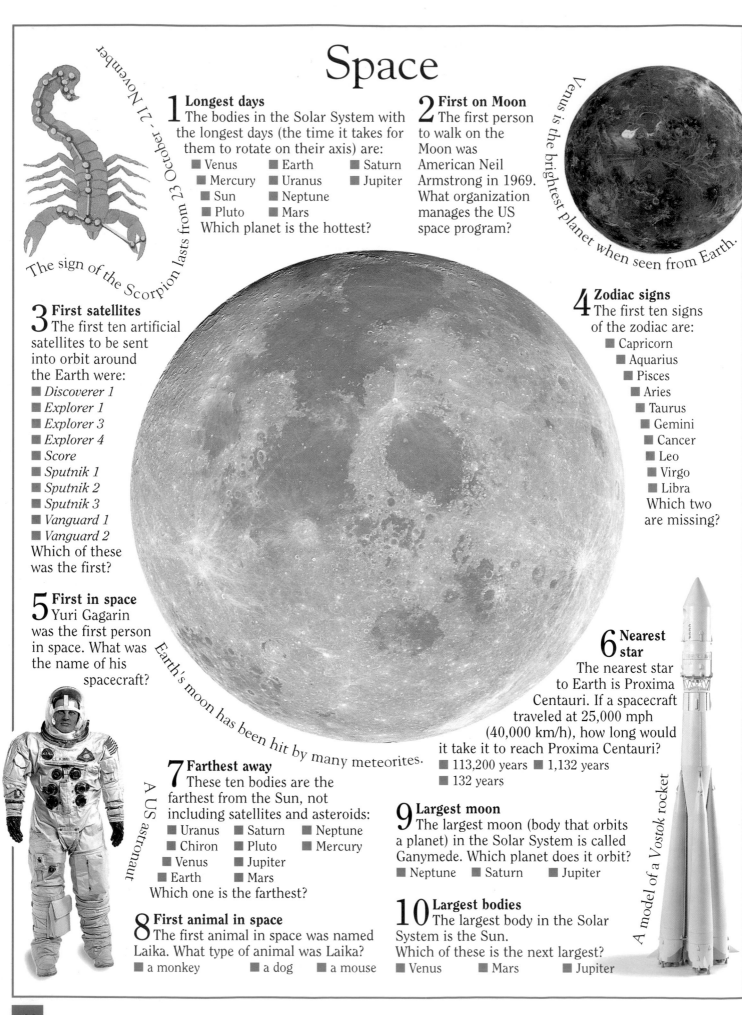

1 Longest days
The bodies in the Solar System with the longest days (the time it takes for them to rotate on their axis) are:
- Venus
- Earth
- Saturn
- Mercury
- Uranus
- Jupiter
- Sun
- Neptune
- Pluto
- Mars

Which planet is the hottest?

2 First on Moon
The first person to walk on the Moon was American Neil Armstrong in 1969. What organization manages the US space program?

Venus is the brightest planet when seen from Earth.

3 First satellites
The first ten artificial satellites to be sent into orbit around the Earth were:
- *Discoverer 1*
- *Explorer 1*
- *Explorer 3*
- *Explorer 4*
- *Score*
- *Sputnik 1*
- *Sputnik 2*
- *Sputnik 3*
- *Vanguard 1*
- *Vanguard 2*

Which of these was the first?

4 Zodiac signs
The first ten signs of the zodiac are:
- Capricorn
- Aquarius
- Pisces
- Aries
- Taurus
- Gemini
- Cancer
- Leo
- Virgo
- Libra

Which two are missing?

5 First in space
Yuri Gagarin was the first person in space. What was the name of his spacecraft?

Earth's moon has been hit by many meteorites.

A US astronaut

6 Nearest star
The nearest star to Earth is Proxima Centauri. If a spacecraft traveled at 25,000 mph (40,000 km/h), how long would it take it to reach Proxima Centauri?
- 113,200 years
- 1,132 years
- 132 years

7 Farthest away
These ten bodies are the farthest from the Sun, not including satellites and asteroids:
- Uranus
- Saturn
- Neptune
- Chiron
- Pluto
- Mercury
- Venus
- Jupiter
- Earth
- Mars

Which one is the farthest?

8 First animal in space
The first animal in space was named Laika. What type of animal was Laika?
- a monkey
- a dog
- a mouse

9 Largest moon
The largest moon (body that orbits a planet) in the Solar System is called Ganymede. Which planet does it orbit?
- Neptune
- Saturn
- Jupiter

10 Largest bodies
The largest body in the Solar System is the Sun. Which of these is the next largest?
- Venus
- Mars
- Jupiter

A model of a *Vostok* rocket

Weather

Weathervanes are turned by the wind.

The sun casts a shadow on the face of a sundial.

1 Greatest snowstorm
The greatest snowstorm was at Mt. Shasta in California from February 13–19, 1959. About 192 in (4,800 mm) of snow fell. Is it true that no two snowflakes are the same?

2 Windiest place
In Commonwealth Bay, Antarctica, winds can reach up to 200 mph (320 km/h). What does a weathervane tell us about the wind?

3 Wettest location
The wettest place in the world is Mawsynram, India. What do scientists use to measure rainfall?

4 Most rainy days
Mt. Wai-'ale-'ale in Hawaii has more rainy days than anywhere else with as many as 350 rainy days per year. A barometer is used to show what type of weather to expect. What does it measure?

- temperature
- air pressure
- wind velocity

The pointer in a barometer moves because of air pressure.

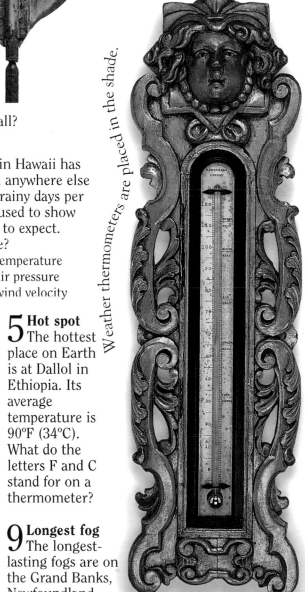

Weather thermometers are placed in the shade.

5 Hot spot
The hottest place on Earth is at Dallol in Ethiopia. Its average temperature is 90°F (34°C). What do the letters F and C stand for on a thermometer?

6 Heaviest hailstorm
The heaviest hailstones fell in Gopalganj, Bangladesh, in 1985. The hailstones weighed up to 2.2 lb (1 kg), as much as a bag of sugar. Is hail made of frozen rain or frozen water vapor?

7 Least sunshine
The South Pole has the least sunshine, with darkness for 182 days of the year. What instrument uses the sun to tell the time?

Snowflakes are a collection of ice crystals frozen together.

8 Thunderstorms
Tororo, Uganda, has more thunder than anywhere else in the world. Thunder is heard there on an average of 251 days a year. What is often seen when there is thunder?

9 Longest fog
The longest-lasting fogs are on the Grand Banks, Newfoundland, Canada. They can last for weeks. What do you call fog that forms over cities and is caused by polluted air?

10 Coldest temperature
The coldest temperature ever recorded is -129°F (-89°C) at Vostok Station. Is Vostok in the Arctic or the Antarctic?

A rain gauge catches rain in a funnel.

Countries of the world

The Eiffel Tower rises 984 ft (300 m) above Paris.

Australia was once part of the British Empire.

A red London double-decker bus

1 Most neighbors
Which of these countries is the nation with the most neighboring countries?
- ■ Saudi Arabia
- ■ Russia
- ■ China

2 Smallest country
The smallest country in the world is Vatican City.
What famous person lives there?

3 Largest country
The ten largest countries in the world are:
- ■ Russia
- ■ Canada
- ■ China
- ■ US
- ■ Brazil
- ■ Australia
- ■ India
- ■ Argentina
- ■ Kazakhstan
- ■ Sudan

Four of these countries' flags are shown on these two pages. Which are they?

4 Most tourists
Countries with the most tourists each year are:
- ■ France
- ■ Spain
- ■ US
- ■ Italy
- ■ China
- ■ UK
- ■ Hungary
- ■ Mexico
- ■ Poland
- ■ Austria

To which country would tourists go to visit the Eiffel Tower?

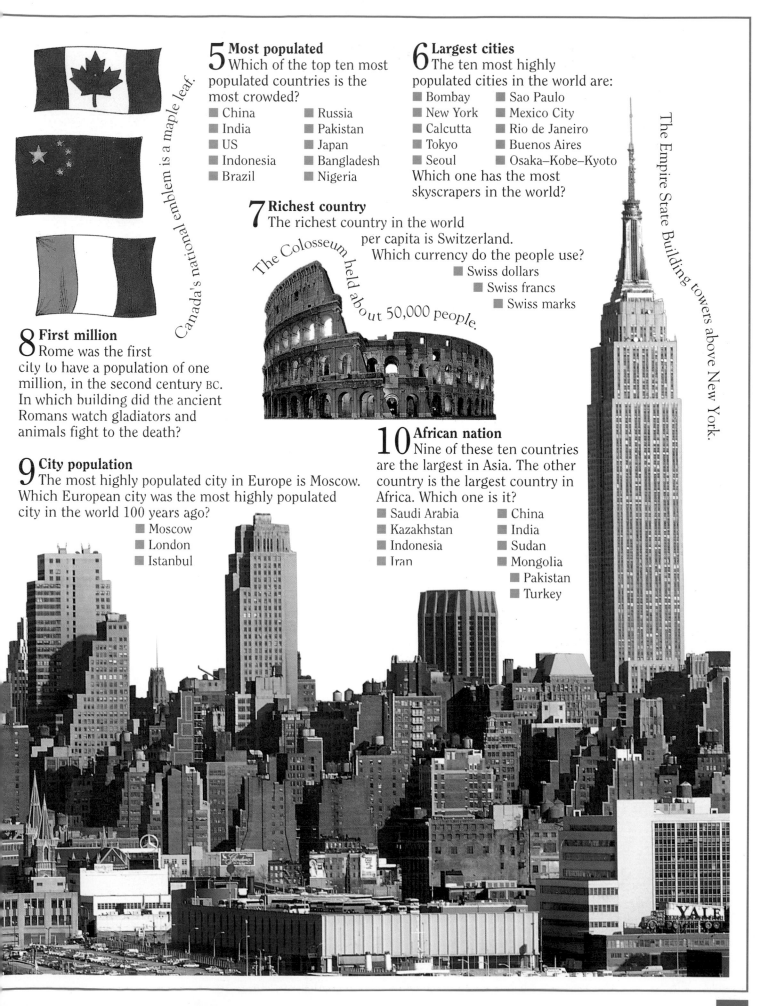

Canada's national emblem is a maple leaf.

5 Most populated
Which of the top ten most populated countries is the most crowded?

- China
- India
- US
- Indonesia
- Brazil
- Russia
- Pakistan
- Japan
- Bangladesh
- Nigeria

6 Largest cities
The ten most highly populated cities in the world are:

- Bombay
- New York
- Calcutta
- Tokyo
- Seoul
- Sao Paulo
- Mexico City
- Rio de Janeiro
- Buenos Aires
- Osaka–Kobe–Kyoto

Which one has the most skyscrapers in the world?

7 Richest country
The richest country in the world per capita is Switzerland. Which currency do the people use?

- Swiss dollars
- Swiss francs
- Swiss marks

The Colosseum held about 50,000 people.

8 First million
Rome was the first city to have a population of one million, in the second century BC. In which building did the ancient Romans watch gladiators and animals fight to the death?

9 City population
The most highly populated city in Europe is Moscow. Which European city was the most highly populated city in the world 100 years ago?

- Moscow
- London
- Istanbul

10 African nation
Nine of these ten countries are the largest in Asia. The other country is the largest country in Africa. Which one is it?

- Saudi Arabia
- Kazakhstan
- Indonesia
- Iran
- China
- India
- Sudan
- Mongolia
- Pakistan
- Turkey

The Empire State Building towers above New York.

Disasters

An earthquake under the sea may cause a huge wave.

1 Worst tsunami
The worst tsunami in the world was in the Atlantic Ocean in 1775. It hit Morocco, western Africa, killing 60,000 people. What is a tsunami?

This large jet can carry up to 550 passengers.

2 Avalanche disaster
The worst avalanche of the 20th century killed over 18,000 people in the mountains of Peru in 1970. Were the victims buried under:
- sand
- snow
- soil

4 Oil spill
The worst oil spill happened when two ships collided off the coast of Trinidad in 1979. 330,700 tons (300,000 tonnes) of oil were spilled. What are ships that transport oil called?

Buildings can collapse when the Earth's crust moves.

3 Fireworks
The worst fireworks disaster occured at the royal wedding of the Dauphin in 1770 in Paris, France. Up to 800 people were killed. Who was the Dauphin?

5 Sports disaster
The worst disaster at a sports venue was the collapse of a spectators' stand at the Hong Kong Jockey Club in 1918, killing 604 people. What sport takes place there?
- show jumping
- horse racing
- track and field

8 Volcanic eruption
In 1815, 92,000 people were killed when Tambora, Indonesia, erupted in the worst ever volcano eruption. What is the red-hot material that flows from a volcano called?

Some lava cools to look like a coil of rope.

6 Hurricanes
The most damaging hurricane was Hurricane Andrew in 1992. How does a hurricane get its name?

Snow sometimes slips down steep mountain slopes.

7 Rail disaster
The worst rail disaster was in India in 1981. About 800 people died when a conductor braked to avoid an animal sacred to followers of Hinduism and the train plunged off a bridge. What animal caused the crash?

9 Earthquake
The worst earthquake killed 1,100,000 people in the Mediterranean in 1202. What scale measures an earthquake?

Ships like this carry oil in tanks.

10 Aircraft disaster
In 1977 a KLM and a Pan Am Boeing 747 crashed in the worst aircraft disaster ever. What nickname is given to Boeing 747s?

Buildings

1 Tallest building
Petronas Towers in Kuala Lumpur, Southeast Asia is claimed to be the tallest building in the world. What are tall buildings often called?

2 Lived-in castle
The largest inhabited castle is Windsor Castle in England. What is the wall on top of a castle that is alternately high and low called?

3 Tallest structure
The Warszawa Radio Mast in Poland was once the world's tallest structure. Why does it no longer hold the record?

4 Largest palace
The largest palace is the Forbidden City in Beijing, China. Who used to live there?

Builders stand on platforms made from planks and poles.

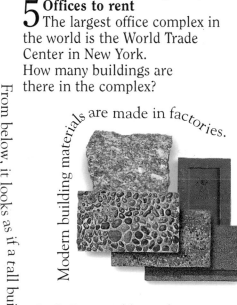

The Forbidden City is also known as the Imperial City.

5 Offices to rent
The largest office complex in the world is the World Trade Center in New York. How many buildings are there in the complex?

6 Ground area
The Pentagon in Washington, DC covers the largest ground area of any office building. It also has the largest telephone switchboard. How many phone lines does it have?
- 345
- 3,450
- 34,500

The Skydome with its roof open

7 Tallest tower
The world's tallest self-supporting tower is the CN Tower in Toronto, Canada. What framework do builders use to put up a tall building?

8 Costly house
The most expensive private house ever built is the Hearst Ranch in California. Are most modern houses built from natural or artificial materials?

9 Sports stadium
The largest covered stadium is the Aztec Stadium in Mexico City. Who were the Aztecs?

From below, it looks as if a tall building touches the sky.

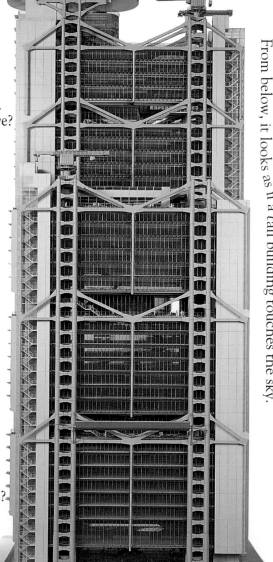

Modern building materials are made in factories.

10 Retractable roof
The building with the largest retractable roof is the Toronto Skydome in Canada, the home of the Blue Jays baseball team. What can the roof be made to do?

The top of the castle was a strong defense point.

Deserts

The desert rose stores water in its fleshy stems and leaves.

1 Largest desert
Which of these 10 deserts is the largest?
- Arabian, Arabia
- Gobi, Mongolia
- Somali, Somalia
- Namib, Namibia
- Sonoran, Mexico
- Takla Makam, China
- Australian, Central Australia
- Kalahari, Southern Africa
- Sahara, Northern Africa
- Turkestan, Central Asia

Rattlesnakes live in dry areas of North and Central America

2 Largest cactus
The largest cactus in the world is the saguaro, which grows in Arizona and California, and also in Mexico. How does the cactus survive without water in the desert?

3 Giant stone
The Simpson Desert in Australia contains the largest exposed block of stone in the world.
Is this called:
- Uluru
- Giant's Causeway
- Ship Rock

Tuareg nomads wear silver crosses for protection.

4 Ancient pyramid
The oldest surviving pyramid is in the desert at Saqqara, in Egypt. It was built in 2680 BC as a tomb for the ruler of ancient Egypt. What are the rulers of ancient Egypt called?

5 Longest drought
Which desert had the longest drought in recorded history?
- The Atacama Desert
- The Gobi Desert
- The Namib Desert

Fierce winds often blow across desert

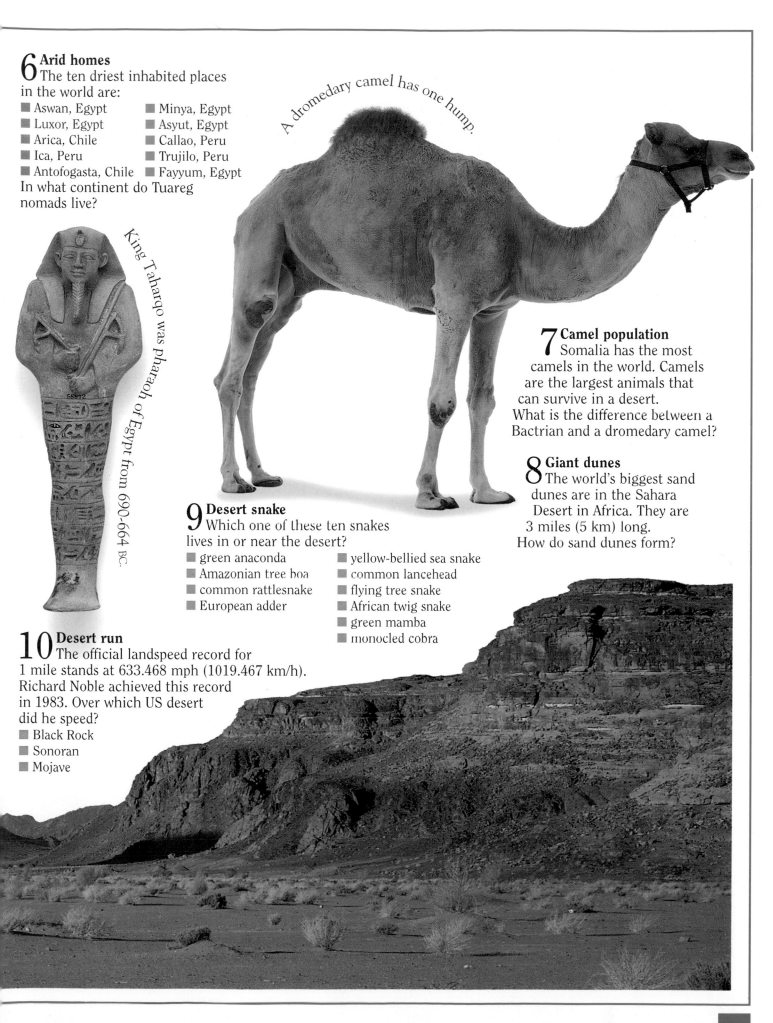

6 Arid homes
The ten driest inhabited places in the world are:
- Aswan, Egypt
- Luxor, Egypt
- Arica, Chile
- Ica, Peru
- Antofogasta, Chile
- Minya, Egypt
- Asyut, Egypt
- Callao, Peru
- Trujilo, Peru
- Fayyum, Egypt

In what continent do Tuareg nomads live?

A dromedary camel has one hump.

King Taharqo was pharaoh of Egypt from 690-664 BC.

7 Camel population
Somalia has the most camels in the world. Camels are the largest animals that can survive in a desert.
What is the difference between a Bactrian and a dromedary camel?

8 Giant dunes
The world's biggest sand dunes are in the Sahara Desert in Africa. They are 3 miles (5 km) long.
How do sand dunes form?

9 Desert snake
Which one of these ten snakes lives in or near the desert?
- green anaconda
- Amazonian tree boa
- common rattlesnake
- European adder
- yellow-bellied sea snake
- common lancehead
- flying tree snake
- African twig snake
- green mamba
- monocled cobra

10 Desert run
The official landspeed record for 1 mile stands at 633.468 mph (1019.467 km/h). Richard Noble achieved this record in 1983. Over which US desert did he speed?
- Black Rock
- Sonoran
- Mojave

Answers

The human body

1 Largest organ
Heart. Barnard (1922–) is a South African surgeon. He became famous after he transplanted the heart of a dead patient into Louis Washkansky, who survived 18 days.

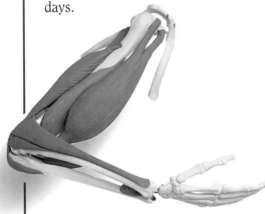

2 Longest bones
The femur. The second and third longest bones in your body, the tibia and fibula, are also in your leg. They run from the knee to the ankle. The tibia is your shin bone. The fibula is slightly behind it.

3 Oldest men
Women (see question 10). The average life expectancy for men in Japan is 76.1 years. In most developing countries, particularly those in Africa, the average age is no more than 45 years. In Sierra Leone it is only 41.4 years.

4 Sports injuries
Muscles. The human body contains 650 muscles, which carry out all the body's movements. When a muscle is strained, it is torn, causing swelling and bleeding.

5 Common accidents
Endoscope. This instrument allows a doctor to see inside the body without having to operate. One can, for example, insert an endoscope down a patient's throat right into their body to examine the inside of the stomach.

6 Visits to the doctor
High blood pressure. This is measured using two figures. The first gives the pressure as the heart pumps blood into the system; the second gives the pressure when the heart rests between beats.

7 Common reaction
No. Only the female of many wasps and bees has a stinger. It is an adaptation of a bee's egg-laying apparatus. It is used to inject poison into a victim, causing a painful wound. Some people react more than others to being stung.

8 Food reaction
A food allergy. If someone has an allergy to something it may cause anything from a slight rash to death. Nuts are especially dangerous to some people.

9 Common fears
Spiders. A phobia is a great fear of something, and "arachno" comes from the scientific name for the class to which spiders belong – Arachnida.

10 Longest-living women
More than 80 years. Life expectancy throughout the world has gradually become longer. In the 5th century, women were expected to live for only 27 years.

People

1 Female premiers
Indira Gandhi. Mrs. Gandhi was prime minister of India from 1966–77 and 1980–84. Her son Rajiv became prime minister after her, but he, too, was assassinated, in 1989 during the campaign leading up to a general election.

2 Longest reign
Crown jewels. These officially consist of items such as crowns and orbs, which are used by royalty in ceremonies and on state occasions. The British Crown Jewels are kept in the Tower of London.

3 Wealthy people
Millionaires. The word was first used in about 1826. A person who has more than one billion dollars is called a billionaire.

4 Roman emperors
Tiberius. He was emperor of Rome from AD 14–37. He was the stepson of Augustus, who chose him to be his successor because there was no other suitable person.

5 First president
George Washington. He was Commander-in-Chief of the American army during the Revolutionary War. The Americans won the war in 1781, and the United States of America was recognized as an independent nation in 1783.

6 Duty free
Duty free means that tax payment is not owed to the government on the import or export of items such as cigarettes, perfume, and alcohol. The items are therefore cheaper than at home, where duty has to be paid. People can buy duty-free items at an airport or on an airplane.

7 Stressful job
The First Lady. She attends official occasions with the president and often travels with him on official visits to other countries. She also has her own staff and functions to attend to.

8 Litter
Yes, it is true that chewing gum is illegal in Singapore. This is because it is thought to be a dirty habit that lowers the standards of the country.

9   Walking at work
Australia. The Royal Flying Doctor Service was started in 1928, carrying doctors by air to patients in places difficult to reach by road.

10   Top of the world
May. Most mountaineers that climb Mt. Everest do so in May because the weather is better for climbing during this month.

Food and drink

1   Mushroom farming
France. On average, the people in France eat 6.97 lb (3.17 kg) of mushrooms each in a year.

2   Sweet tooth
Sugarcane. This is a type of grass that grows up to 13 ft (4 m) high. When the stems are crushed, a sugary juice emerges. Sugarcane is cultivated in tropical and sub-tropical areas of the world.

3   Ice-cream nation
Sunday. It is possible that any ice-cream left over at the end of the week was sold on Sundays mixed with other ingredients, and this is how a sundae got its name.

4   Cheese producer
Cheese is made from milk. The milk forms lumps, and then the lumps, called curds, are separated from the watery part of the milk. They are then pressed, shaped into molds, and left in a warm place to ripen.

5   Tea drinkers
India. Tea leaves are made from the young leaves and shoots of tea bushes. The leaves are taken to a factory where they are withered, rolled, and fermented.

6   Food crops
Most bread is made from wheat, the grains of which are ground to make flour. Bread is usually made from a mixture of flour, salt, water, and yeast to make it rise.

7   Fruit quantities
Seeds. These are produced inside the fruit of a plant, then scattered in one of a number of ways. When the conditions are right, the seeds will germinate and grow roots and stems.

8   Coffee drinkers
No, it is not true. Coffee is made from the seeds of the coffee tree. They are roasted and ground before they are brewed in hot water to make the drink.

9   Oldest cake
In a grave. The cake is 4.4 in (11 cm) wide, has sesame on it, and honey inside it. It is now in a museum of food in Vevey, Switzerland.

10   Expensive wine
France. When referring to wine, the term "château," which means "castle" in French, refers to the property where the wine was made. It does not mean there is a castle.

Art and culture

1   Shakespeare's longest
The Globe Theatre. This famous Elizabethan theater was near the Thames River in London. It burned down in 1613 during a performance of *Henry VIII*, but was rebuilt the following year. It was finally demolished in 1644.

2   Youngest Oscar winners
Six. Shirley Temple won a special award and was presented with a miniature Oscar, as were 11 other young stars. Tatum O'Neal is the youngest winner of a major award – Best Supporting Actress 1973 – for her role in *Paper Moon*. She was 10 years old.

3   Top-selling album
Michael Jackson. Other top selling albums of all time include the Beatles' *Sgt. Pepper's Lonely Hearts Club Band*, Bruce Springsteen's *Born in the USA*, and the soundtrack to *The Sound of Music*.

4   Best-seller
It was the first Bible to be printed using movable type. Johannes Gutenberg (1398–1468) was a German printer. He invented a printing press in 1428 on which he could print several copies, or impressions, of the same page.

5   Popular language
China. Mandarin is now the standard language taught all over China, but there are four other languages spoken in China: Wu Cantonese, Min, and Hakka.

6   Best-selling newspapers
Their size. A tabloid newspaper is half the size of a broadsheet newspaper.

7   Top animation
Pocahontas. Pocahontas (1595–1617) was the daughter of the chief of the Powhatan tribe in North America. She saved the life of an English man, John Smith, when he was captured by the tribe.

8   Priceless painting
Yes. Dr. Gachet was also van Gogh's patron. Van Gogh (1853–90) went to stay with him in 1890, but he suffered from hallucinations and depression and shot himself the same year.

9   Largest library
A paperback. The Library of Congress was founded in 1800. As well as books, it houses pamphlets, manuscripts, photographs, maps, and music.

10   First television service
John Logie Baird (1888–1946). In 1926, Baird, a Scottish inventor, demonstrated his television by showing the first recognizable pictures of a human face. His pictures, with added sound, were transmitted in 1930.

Transportation

1 Longest ship
Liners. They are called liners because a company that owns a collection of ships is called a shipping line. Airliners are airplanes that belong to airlines.

2 Best-seller
John Dunlop. The pneumatic tire was originally invented by Robert W. Thomson in 1845 for use on carriages. It was reinvented by Dunlop in 1887 while he was working as a vet.

3 Longest rail network
The United States. The largest station is Grand Central Terminal in New York, built between 1903–13. It covers 48 acres (19 ha) on two levels. There are 41 tracks on the upper level and 26 on the lower level. About 550 trains use the station every day.

4 First car
Spark plugs. Most cars are powered by a gasoline engine. An electric spark from a spark plug makes a mixture of gasoline and air explode. The hot gases produced push a piston down, which turns the car's wheels.

5 First motor race
Ferrari. The company was started in 1929 by Enzo Ferrari (1898–1988), an Italian race car driver. Today the company produces race cars and sports cars for the road.

6 Longest road tunnel
The Alps. Work on the road tunnel was started in 1969 and was completed in 1980. It is 10 miles (16 km) long and goes from Goschenen to Airolo in Switzerland.

7 First airplane
The Concorde. Its first passenger flight was on January 21, 1976. The Concorde cruises at 1,458 mph (2,333 km/h). It holds the record for the fastest flight between New York and London at 2 hr 54 min 30 sec, set on April 14, 1990.

8 International airport
John Fitzgerald Kennedy. The airport handles about 15 million international passengers a year. Chicago's O'Hare airport is the busiest of all the airports in the world, handling more than 65 million passengers a year.

9 Motorcycle first
Mopeds have pedals. Their engine is usually only 50 cc (cubic centimeters), whereas motorcycles can have an engine of more than 1,500 cc. A moped can be thought of as an engine-assisted bicycle.

10 Road network
The United States and Canada. The road is the Pan-American Highway. It is over 15,000 miles (24,140 km) long.

Religion

1 Buddhist population
China. Buddhism originated in India in the 6th century BC. Its teaching of peace and tolerant coexistence appealed to many people and the religion spread through Asia and beyond.

2 Islamic nation
Indonesia. Muslims follow the religion of Islam. They believe in one god, Allah, whose messenger is Muhammad. Islam originated in Mecca, in present-day Saudi Arabia, where Muhammad was born. Mecca is therefore the most sacred place in the Muslim world.

3 Biblical blockbusters
The Ten Commandments. This film, starring Charlton Heston as Moses and Yul Brynner as Pharaoh, was directed by Cecil B. DeMille and released in 1956. It is almost 4 hours long.

4 Hindu population
India. Most Hindus believe in many gods, but in one underlying reality. They believe that when a person dies, his or her soul is reborn in another body. People who lead a good life are reborn to a higher life; people who lead a bad life are reborn to a lower life.

5 Bible animals
Sheep. They are mentioned 200 times in the Bible and lambs are mentioned 188 times.

6 World religions
Christianity. This religion has an estimated 1,900,174,000 followers around the world. Christians believe that Jesus Christ is the Son of God.

7 Jewish population
United States. There are Jewish communities in almost every country. Their faith is called Judaism. It originated in about 2000 BC. For Jews, the Promised Land is Israel, in the Middle East.

8 Names of popes
John. There have been 23 Pope Johns. The Pope is the Bishop of Rome. He is considered by Roman Catholics to be the successor to St. Peter, Jesus' closest disciple.

9 Largest religious structure
Angkor Wat. This temple, dedicated to the Hindu god Vishnu, was built in 1113–1150. It encloses an area of 402 acres (162.6 ha) and once had a population of 80,000.

10 Christian countries
The United States. There are Christian communities all over the world. The main branches of Christianity are: Roman Catholic, Protestant, and Eastern Orthodox.

Extinct animals

1 Longest dinosaur
Diplodocus ate plants. It may have fed around the edges of ponds where the water would have helped support its great weight. It lived about 145 million years ago.

2 Longest neck
30 ft (9 m). *Mamenchisaurus*'s long neck was made up of 19 vertebrae. The animal used its neck to reach food. Its neck could probably only bend at the head and shoulder.

3 Tallest dinosaur
Because it had particularly long front legs. A complete skeleton, made from several individuals, is on display in Berlin. It measures 19.7 ft (6 m) high at the shoulder.

4 Smallest brain
Rows of plates down its back. The plates extended up its neck and down its tail. *Stegosaurus* also had four spikes at the end of its tail.

5 Largest meat eater
King of the tyrant lizards. *Tyrannosaurus rex* measured up to 49 ft (15 m) long and up to 20 ft (6 m) high. It had curved teeth for tearing meat, and a powerful neck to hold up its large head.

6 Smallest dinosaur
A chicken. *Compsognathus* was only about 28 in (70 cm) long. Its name means "pretty jaw" because the first skeleton, found in the 1850s, was such a beautiful specimen. *Wannanosaurus* may only have measured 24 in (60 cm) in length.

7 Prehistoric elephant
A mammoth. Woolly mammoths stood about 10 ft (3 m) at the shoulders. They became extinct about 4,000 years ago.

8 Recently extinct
A dodo. This flightless bird became extinct in the late 1700s, about 100 years after it was discovered. It was about as large as a turkey, with curly tail feathers and a hooked beak.

9 Tallest bird
The ostrich. The moa lived in New Zealand. It could not fly, but was not threatened by predators. The largest species of moa was 11.5 ft (3.5 m) tall.

10 Flying creature
A reptile. It was a pterosaur (winged reptile) that lived in the late Cretaceous period in present-day Texas.

Domestic animals

1 Oldest horse
Its teeth. The cutting edge of a horse's front teeth wears down with age. This helps in estimating the age of a horse.

2 Heaviest rooster
A cockerel. Chickens were domesticated about 8,000 years ago. There are 150 different breeds, all descended from the red jungle fowl of Southeast Asia.

3 Smallest horse
Falabella. This breed originated in Argentina. The first ones were crosses between the smallest Shetland ponies and small thoroughbreds. It is classified as a horse, not a pony.

4 Smallest dog
2.5 in (6.3 cm). This tiny dog measured 3.8 in (9.5 cm) from the tip of its nose to the root of its tail and weighed only 4 oz (113 g).

5 Breeding like rabbits
A kitten. A female rabbit is a doe and a male rabbit is a buck.

6 Top cat
Because it behaves like one. When they are stroked, Ragdoll cats become extremely relaxed and go limp like ragdolls.

7 Smallest pig
A sow. A male pig is called a boar. Mini Maialinos were developed in Italy. Piglets weigh only 14 oz (400 g) at birth.

8 Heavy hound
The mastiff. This ancient breed of dog is renowned for its great courage and guarding instincts. There are many accounts through the ages of mastiffs in battle.

9 Sheep station
70,000. This sheep station (called Commonwealth Hill) covers an area of 4,080 sq miles (10,567 sq km), enclosed by 138 miles (221 km) of fencing.

10 Dwarf rabbit
Larger (see question 4). Wild rabbits are all about the same size. Pet rabbits can come in many sizes, from dwarf to giant.

Birds

1 Largest feathers
The crested argus. A type of pheasant, the male's tail feathers are more than 6 in (15 cm) wide and 59 in (150 cm) long. He displays his tail and wing feathers when courting a female pheasant.

2 Pet parrots
The kakapo. There are probably less than 40 of these flightless birds left. They live in New Zealand, but mammals such as cats have devastated the population.

3 Songbirds
The red-billed quelea. These small African songbirds eat mostly seeds, and feed in flocks of more than one million individuals.

4 Wingspan
The wandering albatross. This huge seabird has a wingspan of about 9.8 ft (3 m). It is a powerful flyer and comes to land only to nest.

5 Big bird
The great bustard. This long-necked bird breeds in grassland areas of Europe, Asia, and northern Africa. A male bird can weigh as much as 42 lb (19 kg).

6 Long life
The oystercatcher. This bird can live to be more than 35 years old. It breeds in northern Europe and Asia. In winter, it flies south as far as Africa, India, and southern China.

7 Birds of prey
The peregrine falcon. It can dive at up to 185 mph (298 km/h), which is the greatest speed reached by any bird.

8 Smallest bird
The bee hummingbird. This Cuban bird weighs only 0.05 oz (1.6 g) and measures just 3 in (7.5 cm) long. This is smaller than many butterflies.

9 Largest bird
The ostrich. It lives in Africa and stands at an average height of 8.2 ft (2.5 m). It cannot fly, but it has large, strong legs that enable it to run at 40 mph (64 km/h).

10 Migration
The Arctic tern. It raises its young in the Arctic summer, flying to the Antarctic in fall, to winter there. Then it flies back again for summer in the Arctic. This is a round trip of about 25,000 miles (40,000 km).

Animal records

1 Longest snake
The reticulated python. Most grow to more than 20.5 ft (6.25 m). These pythons live in Southeast Asia, Indonesia, and the Philippines.

2 Most endangered
The Tasmanian wolf. The last known died in a zoo in 1936, but since then there have been a few unconfirmed sightings.

3 Largest carnivore
The North American brown bear. There are about 50,000 brown bears in North America. The Kodiak bear, from Kodiak Island in Alaska, is the largest. An adult can weigh more than 1,320 lb (600 kg).

4 Rarest marine mammal
The Mediterranean monk seal. This species of seal used to be found throughout the Mediterranean, the Black Sea, and the west of North Africa. Today there are no more than 500 seals worldwide.

5 Animal class
Amphibians. The word "amphibian" comes from the Greek words *amphi* and *bios*, meaning "double life." Amphibians can live on land and in water.

6 Longest animal
The crocodile. Crocodiles belong to the same group of animals that included the dinosaurs and the ancestors of birds.

7 Longest living
The giant tortoise. This is also the largest living tortoise. A male on Bird Island, in the Seychelles, weighed 668 lb (304 kg).

8 Fastest mammal
66 mph (105 km/h). A cheetah can keep up this speed over 1,310 ft (400 m).

9 Largest litter
The African hunting dog. The pack is led by the strongest and bravest individuals. Once a hunting pack is within 1,640 ft (500 m) of its prey, the animals begin to stalk.

10 Laziest creatures
The armadillo. Armadillos were named by Spanish soldiers when they invaded South America in the 16th century. They sleep for an average of 19 hours a day.

Insects and spiders

1 Loudest insect
On either side of their body. Cicadas have been famous throughout history for the songs the males use to attract females.

2 Insect migration
By day. Butterflies and moths have large, delicate wings with which they fly skillfully, at about 5.5 mph (9 km/h).

3 Largest insect
Worldwide Fund for Nature (WWF). Its famous emblem is a giant panda.

4 Fastest insect
Two. However, true flies are insects that have only one pair of wings. The other pair has been reduced to sticklike organs that the flies use for balancing.

5 Giant webs
Special silken thread that the spider produces itself. Orb spiders make two types of threads in different thicknesses – a thick one for the frame of the web, and a thinner one for the center.

6 Largest spider
Spiders have eight legs; insects have six. Spiders belong to the class of animals Arachnida.

7 Heaviest insect
Yes. Large beetles like the Goliath beetle have to take off from a plant because they are too heavy to lift themselves off the ground.

8 Most deadly
With a bite. The species *Phoneutria fera* is the most poisonous of all. It is aggressive, and if disturbed in its hiding-place, it will bite angrily.

9 Longest insect
Because it looks like a twig. The legs of this insect are so long that when it sheds its skin, the legs often get trapped. For this reason, stick insects often have legs missing.

10 Insect towers
The mounds are built so that fresh air can circulate. Some termites build their nests with air-conditioning. Air travels around, getting cooled as it moves down flues near the edge of the nest.

Reptiles

1 Longest lizard
Shed their tail. Many lizards can do this as a form of defense. The tail breaks off along a special crack in the bones. The lizard then grows a new tail.

2 Fastest snake
Most snakes wriggle along. They do this by throwing their body into curves and pushing backward with the curves on the ground.

3 Giant fangs
By poisoning it with venom. The gaboon viper injects the poison into its prey through tubes in its front fangs. The fangs are so long that they are folded away when not in use.

4 Largest turtle
It is not hard, but leathery. Most turtles and tortoises have a domed shell across their back to protect their soft body. The leatherback turtle breeds in the Caribbean before following its main food, jellyfish, across the Atlantic Ocean.

5 Smallest reptile
A lizard. Geckos are found in all warm countries. They are expert climbers and can run upside down across ceilings in pursuit of prey.

6 Largest lizard
Yes. The Komodo dragon is a type of lizard called a monitor. It lives on several Indonesian islands, including Komodo. Adult dragons live on the pigs and deer native to the islands, and also the goats introduced by humans.

7 Egg laying
On the beach. The female crawls out of the sea at night. She digs a pit above the high-tide mark with her flipper and lays her eggs. The young have to fend for themselves from the moment they hatch.

8 Old reptile
152 years old. It was brought to Mauritius from the Seychelles in 1766. It went blind in 1908 and was accidentally killed in 1918.

9 Largest reptile
Rivers and swamps. Alligators, caimans, gharials, and crocodiles all belong to the same group of animals.

10 Smallest snake
It is shed. Snakes have to shed their skins every so often as they grow. They have a new skin underneath. Most snakes shed their skin in a single piece.

Plant life

1 Deadly fungus
6–15 hours. The yellowish-green death cap grows in Britain. If you ate one, you would suffer vomiting, delirium, collapse, and death.

2 Tallest grass
The giant panda. Pandas have to eat at least 44 lb (20 kg) of bamboo a day to get enough energy from it to keep going. When they are not eating or looking for food, they sleep to save energy.

3 Largest bloom
Because it smells horrible. It actually smells like rotting flesh, which attracts insects for pollination. The plant flowers only once every ten years.

4 Largest seed
Coco-de-mer. This plant is also known as the giant fan palm, or double coconut.

5 Seaweed leaves
More than 35. Pacific giant kelp grows fast. It can grow 18 in (45 cm) in a day.

6 Largest fruiting body
A fungus. Fungi such as toadstools and mushrooms are not plants. Unlike plants, they cannot make their own food using sunlight because they do not contain chlorophyll. They take their food from other plants and animals.

7 Rare fir
No, fir trees are evergreen and do not drop their leaves in fall. They are a type of conifer with tough needlelike leaves. Each leaf lives for a few years, then falls off.

8 Oldest species
The maidenhair tree. It first appeared about 160 million years ago in present-day China.

9 Towering tree
Cones. The giant sequoia tree has a diameter of 36.4 ft (11.1 m) and a girth of 102.7 ft (31.3 m).

10 Tallest species
True. The Statue of Liberty, including its pedestal, is 305 ft (93 m) tall. The tallest tree ever was an eucalyptus in Australia, reported to have been 435 ft (132.6 m) tall.

Earth

1   Highest mountain
The Himalayas. Mt. Everest is 29,028 ft (8,848 m) high. It is on the border between Nepal and China. The top ten mountains are all higher than 25,600 ft (8,000 m).

2   Largest diamond
A type of mineral. Diamond is the hardest mineral of all. In addition to being prized for their beauty, diamond crystals are also used for drilling through rock, cutting glass, and in surgery.

3   Largest volcano
Molten rock. Under the Earth's crust the rock is so hot it melts. Where the crust is weak, the molten rock bursts through, forming a volcano.

4   Highest waterfalls
Angel Falls in Venezuela. They have a drop of 3,212 ft (979 m). They are named after an American pilot, Jimmy Angel, who found them in 1935.

5   Longest glacier
It is cut away. As a glacier moves down a mountain, it scours out rocks. These are deposited at the end or the sides of the glacier.

6   Highest cliffs
By the sea. When waves crash onto the shore they pound the coast, hurling stones onto the rocks. On high coasts this wears away the slope to form a cliff.

7   Largest islands
Arctic Ocean. Greenland lies within the Arctic Circle and its land mass is permanently covered in ice.

8   Longest rivers
The Nile. It flows through Tanzania, Uganda, Sudan, and Egypt, and is 4,168 miles (6,670 km) long.

9   Largest gorge
Erosion. Rocks can be eroded by water, ice, and weather. All features on the Earth's surface are shaped by erosion.

10   Deepest oceans
Yes. Limestone is composed mainly of calcite, which is usually derived from the broken-up shells and skeletons of animals and plants that lived in the sea.

Space

1   Longest days
Venus. This planet is estimated to have a surface temperature of 864°F (462°C). These measurements were made from two probes – the Soviet *Venera* and the American *Pioneer*.

2   First on the Moon
NASA (National Aeronautics and Space Administration). It operates research stations, controls space flights, and trains astronauts.

3   First satellites
Sputnik 1. This was launched on October 4, 1957. Since then, thousands of satellites have been sent into orbit around Earth for scientific, communications, and military purposes.

4   Zodiac signs
Scorpio and *Sagittarius*. The signs of the zodiac are derived from star constellations through which the Sun appears to travel every year.

5   First in space
Vostok 1. The first flight took place on April 12, 1961. The craft landed 118 minutes after the launch. Gagarin landed separately by parachute after ejecting.

6   Nearest star
More than 113,200 years. Proxima Centauri is 4.22 light-years away. One light year equals 5.9 trillion miles (9.5 trillion km).

7   Farthest away
Pluto. It is 3,692,250,000 miles (5,914,000,000 km) from the Sun. This planet was discovered in 1930. It is also the smallest planet.

8   First animal in space
A dog. Laika was a female Samoyed husky. She died in space in 1957. In 1960, Belka and Strelka, two other Samoyeds, were the first animals to orbit Earth and return safely.

9   Largest moon
Jupiter. Ganymede is one of sixteen satellites that orbit Jupiter. It is thought to have an icy surface about 61 miles (97 km) thick.

10   Largest bodies
Jupiter. It has a diameter of 89,365 miles (142,984 km). Jupiter could contain 1,300 Earths and is the fastest spinning planet in the Solar System.

Weather

1   Greatest snowstorm
Yes, no two snowflakes are the same. Each one is a collection of ice crystals made of frozen water vapor. Ice crystals can be in many shapes, including needles, prisms, columns, and hexagons.

2   Windiest place
Which direction the wind is blowing. A wind is described by the direction from which it comes. For example, a west wind comes from the west.

3   Wettest location
A rain gauge. In a rain gauge, a funnel catches the rain and directs it down into a cylinder. The height of water is the amount, in inches or millimeters, of rain that has fallen.

4 Most rainy days
Air pressure. If air is cold it sinks, pushing down to create a higher pressure on Earth. As the air is squashed, it warms up, bringing fine weather. Warm air rises, creating lower pressure on Earth.

5 Hot spot
Fahrenheit and Centigrade (or Celsius). Water freezes at 32°F (0°C), and boils at 212°F (100°C).

6 Heaviest hailstorm
Frozen rain. Hailstones form inside tall storm clouds that are much warmer at the bottom than the top. Raindrops are tossed up and down and freeze in several layers. When they are too heavy, they fall as hail.

7 Least sunshine
A sundial. This has a face marking the hours. A pointer casts a shadow on the face. As the Earth rotates, the shadow moves around the face, pointing to the time.

8 Thunderstorms
Lightning. A flash of lightning occurs when static electricity

builds up inside a storm cloud. Lightning is extremely hot and makes the air expand very fast, causing thunder.

9 Longest fog
Smog. In cities, the air contains many extra particles because of the smoke released by some industries, cars, and homes. Water vapor condenses on these to form thick, yellow smog.

10 Coldest temperature
The Antarctic. This record temperature was recorded on July 21, 1983.

Countries

1 Most neighbors
China. It has 16 neighbors: Afghanistan, Bhutan, Hong Kong, India, Kazakhstan, Kyrgyzstan, Laos, Macao, Mongolia, Myanmar, Nepal, North Korea, Pakistan, Russia, Tajikistan, and Vietnam.

2 Smallest country
The Pope. Vatican City has an area of 108.7 acres (44 ha). It has its own governor, post office, coinage, and law courts.

3 Largest country
Argentina, Australia, Canada, China. Every country has its own flag.

4 Most tourists
France. The Eiffel Tower was built in Paris, France, in 1887–1889. It was designed for the centennial Paris Exhibition of 1889.

5 Most populated
Bangladesh. It has 841 people per sq km of land (2,178 per sq mile).

6 Largest cities
New York. The word "skyscraper" was first used to describe a building in the 1880s, when the first tall office building of 10 stories or more was built in Chicago, Illinois.

7 Richest country
Swiss francs. Swiss banks are used by rich people from all over the world to escape taxation.

8 First million
The Colosseum. When it first opened, in AD 80, the Colosseum's arena could be filled with water, and "sea battles" were fought by gladiators in small ships.

9 City population
London. A hundred years ago, London had a population of 4,231,431. The most highly populated city in the world today is Tokyo, with a population of 28,447,000.

10 African nation
Sudan. It borders the Red Sea and has an area of 9,674,048 sq miles (2,505,581 sq km).

Disasters

1 Worst tsunami
A tidal wave. It is caused by an earthquake or volcanic eruption under the sea. Where the ocean water is deep, the tsunami may be hardly noticeable, but by the time it reaches the coast, it is capable of causing destruction and death.

2 Avalanche disaster
Snow. On average 150 people are killed by avalanches each year. The 1970 avalanche was triggered by a slab of ice breaking away from one of Peru's highest mountains.

3 Fireworks
The eldest son of the King of France. The Dauphin was heir to the French throne until the monarchy was abolished in 1792, following the French Revolution.

4 Oil spill
Oil tankers. The largest ship in the world is a Norwegian tanker called *Jahre Viking*. Large tankers are called "supertankers."

5 Sports disaster
Horse racing. In this sport highly bred horses are trained and groomed for races. Horse racing is sometimes called the "sport of kings" because of its popularity with royalty.

6 Hurricanes
Names are chosen alphabetically by the World Meteorological Organization.

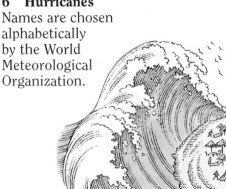

7 Rail disaster
A cow. Cows are considered sacred in Hinduism because they were the companions of Krishna, an incarnation of the god Vishnu. Killing cows is considered a sin by Hindus.

8 Volcanic eruption
Lava. There are two types of lava flows, called aa and pahoehoe. Aa flows are covered in sharp chunks of lava, and pahoehoe lava flows are smooth. Some islands, such as Iceland, are formed by volcanic eruptions.

9 Earthquake
The Richter scale. It measures the energy released during an earthquake. Earthquakes over 8 on the Richter scale can mean the total destruction of an area.

10 Aircraft disaster
Jumbo jet. The Boeing 747 entered commercial service in 1970 as the world's first "wide-bodied jet." The Jumbo jet helped make air travel affordable for everyone.

Buildings

1 Tallest building
Skyscrapers. They were invented in Chicago after the city was destroyed by fire in 1871. With the invention of the elevator, developers could build higher and avoid paying for larger plots.

2 Lived-in castle
Battlements. The battlements protected archers while they were shooting at their enemies.

3 Tallest structure
It fell down during renovation work in 1991. After it collapsed, the local people claimed a new record – that of the world's longest tower!

4 Largest palace
The Emperor of China. It was called the Forbidden City because the palace was so large it seemed like a city, and ordinary people were forbidden from entering it.

5 Offices to rent
Seven. There is a total of 12 million sq ft (1,114,800 sq metres) of rentable space. 50,000 people work in the complex and 70,000 tourists visit every day.

6 Ground area
34,500. The switchboard in the Pentagon, which houses the US Defense Department, handles as many as one million calls per day.

7 Tallest tower
Scaffolding. Early scaffolding was made of wood. Today, it is made of aluminum or steel.

8 Costly house
Artificial materials. In the modern construction industry, parts of buildings are often made away from the building site to save money, space, and time.

9 Sports stadium
An ancient civilization in South America. The Aztecs are famed for their spectacular cities, complex social organization, and golden works of art.

10 Retractable roof
It pulls back to open the stadium to the air. The roof takes about 20 minutes to retract fully.

Deserts

1 Largest desert
The Sahara. This desert covers about 3,579,000 sq miles (9,269,000 sq km). The whole of the United States is only about 40,000 sq miles (100,000 sq km) bigger.

2 Largest cactus
It stores water in its stem. Most cacti avoid losing water through their leaves by having spines instead. Many have very long roots, and collect water when it rains. Their stems can expand to store water.

3 Giant stone
Uluru (formerly known as Ayers Rock). It is 1,142 ft (348 m) high, 1.6 miles (2.5 km) long, and 1 mile (1.6 km) wide, with a circumference of 5.6 miles (9 km).

4 Ancient pyramid
Pharaohs. The Great Pyramids were built as tombs for the pharaohs. Smaller pyramids were built in which to bury important Egyptians.

5 Longest drought
The Atacama Desert in Chile. According to one source, a settlement in the Atacama Desert had no rain for about 400 years.

6 Arid homes
Africa. They have lived in the Sahara Desert of northern Africa since ancient times, although some have now moved to live in towns.

7 Camel population
Bactrian camels have two humps; dromedary camels have one hump. Only Bactrian camels are still found in the wild – in the Gobi Desert.

8 Giant dunes
They are formed by the wind. Dry soils with little vegetation are easily eroded, and in some deserts the wind eventually forms dunes.

9 Desert snake
Common rattlesnakes live in or near deserts in the Americas. They have special heat-sensing pits on each side of their faces that enable them to strike prey accurately in total darkness.

10 Desert run
Black Rock Desert, in Nevada. His car was the Rolls-Royce Avon 302 jet-powered *"Thrust 2,"* designed by John Ackroyd.

Index

Acknowledgments

DK would like to thank:
Mark Haygarth, Iain Morris, and Susan St. Louis for design assistance.
David Pickering for editorial assistance. Special thanks to Miranda Smith for all her help, and Marion Dent for the index.
Additional photography:
Beaulieu; British Museum; Peter Chadwick; Jim Channel; Andy Crawford; Geoff Dann;
Philip Dowell; Mike Dunning; Andreas von Einsiedel; Glasgow Museums;
Frank Greenaway; Marc Henrie; Chas Howson; Colin Keates; Dave King; Kenneth Lilly; Tracy Morgan; National Maritime Museum; Stephen Oliver; Tim Ridley; Science Museum; Karl Shone; James Stevenson; Harry Taylor; Matthew Ward; Jerry Young.
Picture credits
(t=top b=bottom c=center l=left r=right)
AKG London: 8c / Hulton Getty: 8br / NASA: 28tr, c /
Robert Harding Picture Library: 14-15b / Zefa Pictures: 24-25b, 30-31b
Every effort has been made to trace the copyright holders of photographs and we apologize if any omissions have been made.